DAVID WILKERSON:
A Final Warning to America

Conversations compiled and edited
by Nicky Cruz

DOVE Christian Books
Melbourne, Florida

Dedication

This book is dedicated to Dave Wilkerson, my spiritual father and a great servant of God — and to his lovely companion, Gwen.

In my childhood, there was a saying that it was better to give a friend roses now than to wait for his funeral — because he can't smell them then! So, this is my tribute to the man who turned my world around.

I have heard it also said, "*Behind* every great man, there is a woman." But I say, "For every great man, there is a great woman *beside* him." That's what Gwen Wilkerson is, a great lady!

Nicky Cruz

DAVID WILKERSON: A FINAL WARNING TO AMERICA

Dove Christian Books, P.O. Box 36-0122, Melbourne, FL 32936
Cover design by Richard Nakamoto • Editorial work and typographical design by Publications Technologies, Eau Gallie, Florida
Printed in the United States of America

All Scripture references are from the King James Version unless otherwise noted.
Excerpts from the newsletters of Times Square Church are used with permission.
Excerpts from In His Strength, by Gwen Wilkerson, are used with permission.

Special Acknowledgment:
I wish to express my thanks to Barbara Mackery, who checked over the early manuscript of this book and helped me immensely with her insights into the man who is Dave Wilkerson.

TABLE OF CONTENTS

FOREWORD

I had to talk David Wilkerson into letting me do a TV special on his ministry and his new outreach in New York City. I knew he might be reluctant. My wife, Gloria, and I, and Dave and his beautiful wife, Gwen, met for dinner at the Marriott Hotel in the Big Apple's old LaGuardia Airport.

There, I brought up the idea. I had been concerned about some of the things I'd heard people say. Too many people didn't understand the Dave Wilkerson that I know.

I felt it was time to look at some of the controversies surrounding this man of God who has been under such constant public scrutiny. I wanted to answer some of the hard questions about what kind of man Dave Wilkerson really is. And I wanted to look candidly at this complex man who has so stirred up modern Christianity.

It was three decades ago that in his daily prayer time this Pennsylvania country preacher glanced at a *Life* magazine article on teen gang killers and suddenly felt God's strong, urgent call to go tell them about Jesus.

IN HIS OBEDIENCE, Dave propelled an entire generation into the religious revolutions of the 1960s and 1970s — years of righteous tumult in which a whole new set of grievances attached themselves to the spiritual Wittenberg Doors of established Christianity.

At one time or another, the hippie Jesus People, the conservative neo-Pentecostals, the experimenting Charismatics and the witnessing Evangelicals all considered him one of their own — as did the young zealots among the

Assemblies of God, the Southern Baptists, the Catholics, the Episcopalians and the Methodists.

But although Dave left behind Brooklyn's Teen Challenge and his full-time ministry to the street gangs and addicts, his heart remained on New York's compassionless streets where, once, he had confronted a snarling teen gang warlord named Nicky Cruz.

Some things never change.

NO MATTER WHAT DAVE or I have done in this last third of a century, we will always be remembered as the wide-eyed preacher and the sneering street-kid from the best-selling books *The Cross and the Switchblade* and *Run, Baby, Run*. Across the globe and in the video stores near your home, the movie still tells our story, convincing millions that Dave looks like Pat Boone and that I should resemble *CHiPs'* motorcycle cop Erik Estrada, who played me in the film.

Dave was the instrument God used to introduce me to Jesus. I would not be an evangelist today if it wasn't for Dave. So, rather than write a tribute after Dave has gone to be with the Lord, I wanted to tell people what I know about this amazing man and his new, urgent call.

He listened to my proposal and didn't seem to be very excited about it. He hesitated for a moment, then stirred, uneasy in his reluctance.

But it was Gwen at his side who heard what I was really saying and sensed the desire of my heart. She listened. She asked questions. Then turning to her husband, she told him, "It's about time you set the record straight."

"Dave," I said, "After all you've done for me, this is something I want to do for you."

"I believe Nicky is the only one who can do it," said Gwen quietly.

And Dave began to like the idea. He gave his approval and sat with me under the hot TV lights for the intense interviews. The special has aired on a number of stations, including the Trinity Broadcasting Network. The first time it was broadcast, 30 million people were reached.

I have watched my personal copy of the special, then replayed the hours of interviews that didn't make it onto the air because of time constraints. As I did, I began to see that I needed to write a book about David Wilkerson. Not a tribute or even a biography — but perhaps an update. Or possibly a different sort of how-to book: Here's how to obey the Lord. Here's how to give up everything and follow Jesus. Here's how to win the war on drugs. Here's how to survive tomorrow.

So much of this is straight from his mouth and heart that I was moved to write it down into a book — *David Wilkerson: A Final Warning to America.*

Now, after months of work and editing, I pray that the Lord will speak to you through the words of this unique man of God whom some call a prophet of doom ... but whom I know to be an honest seeker who has been given the role of watchman. Gently, lovingly, God has used Dave to warn us to turn from our fear of the days ahead and our laziness — and to fall to our knees.

Don't hope to win the war on drugs with God, he warns. Don't expect God to spare our society from terrible judgment for its unrepentant sin, he warns.

Get on your knees, he warns, and seek the mighty, loving God that so loves us: *Look to Jesus!*

And yearn to know Him.

Nicky Cruz

DAVID WILKERSON:
A Final Warning to America

Section I

The Preacher Returns

Chapter 1

Back
to the
Battlefield

"HEY, HE'S STEALING THAT BABY! Stop him!" cried the middle-aged preacher — pain filling his familiar voice.

Determinedly, David Wilkerson ran down the packed sidewalk of Manhattan's decaying 51st Street after a child-snatcher escaping with a baby in its stroller. Anxiously glancing over his shoulder at Wilkerson, the kidnapper zig-zagged crazily toward grafitti-festooned Eighth Avenue, threading through dodging-but-otherwise-apathetic pedestrians.

Bored prostitutes and grinning teen-age drug pushers looked the other way. A young man with purple splotches on his face cringed in a wheelchair, defensively holding up a cardboard sign: *"Dying of AIDS, Homeless, No Place to Go."*

The infant's cries grew faint over the noise of traffic —
as none of the New Yorkers did anything to halt the crime
in progress.

"Stop him!" pleaded Wilkerson, charging through the
indifferent pack. "That man is stealing that little baby!"

Behind Dave at the corner of Ninth Avenue, the infant's 19-year-old mother gawked, stupefied — pointing
silently as her baby disappeared.

THE CITY OF MY VIOLENT YOUTH is ten times worse
than when Dave and I first clashed on the streets of
Brooklyn — back when I was the infamous Nicky Cruz,
teen warlord of the murderous Mau Maus street gang.

It's as if a new, terrible shadow of evil has overtaken
the violent concrete canyons — far worse than even TV
and movies portray it. The old drug parks are filled with
ranting, seemingly demonized homeless. Empty shells of
vandalized buildings overflow with throwaway girls and
boys prostituting themselves on the brutal streets.

Live sex on stage is advertised on flashing marquees. A
murder occurs every five hours and 258 violent crimes are
reported every day. Cops huddle in their battered cars as
pornography, drugs, AIDS, and sporadic, nerve-shattering
violence rule the night.

Graffiti-defiled billboards whimper the "Just Say No"
mockery of a drug war already lost.

"More babies die of AIDS in this city than any other
city anywhere," says Dave. "They are not only born of
AIDS, they are dying of AIDS, and no matter what the cen-
sus says, this city is facing an army of homeless.

Everywhere you look now, if you come out of the
Lincoln Tunnel or the Holland Tunnel, you see people in
wheelchairs who have been there the past month. You see

emaciated people with their little beggars' cans everywhere — dying in the most heartbreaking ways.

"The hospitals are full," Dave told me. "It's a city with
the highest rents in America and the highest taxes. New
York has the most dangerous school system in the whole
United States.

"Millions of discouraged, angry people live in neighborhoods that the police have written off as 'war zones' —
places the cops won't even go into, day or night."

AS DAVE SPRINTED DOWN the dangerous sidewalk,
the kidnapper paused at Eighth Avenue. A newspaper
vendor and three teen-age boys in athletic jerseys joined
the chase as Dave yelled.

Over the newsstand, a headline screamed "Is NYC
Down for the Count?" above a cartoon of a dazed boxer
sprawled on the floor of an arena. The news story said that
New York City is spinning out of control and that many
people believe that this time it may not survive That
morning, the anchorman of a prominent talk show had
told his national audience: *Don't come to New York City.
It's filthy. It's dirty. It's worse than Calcutta.* "He warned
people to stay out of the city," says Wilkerson "He said he
himself is moving out and doesn't plan to come back."

AS THE KIDNAPPER TURNED up Eighth Avenue, the
baby stroller tipped over. Suddenly Dave and the boys and
the newspaper vendor were all over him, hollering and
pinning him to the sidewalk.

"The baby was strapped in and the strap came up
around its neck and somebody opened the strap," Dave remembers. "Somebody had already called the police."

But what Dave remembers was not the joy of reuniting the hysterical mother and child — nor the accolades of bystanders.

No, what stands out in his memory is how the dazed, drug-addicted mother kept glaring at him — unimpressed and unthankful that he had just rescued her child from untold horror.

Her young, thin face instead was filled with hatred.

"She stuck her finger at me and hissed, 'You get out of this city, you don't belong here. I know who you are,'"

Dave winces as he remembers. "Suddenly, I realized that even Satan knew God was about to do something new on the streets of New York City."

Yes, David Wilkerson is back.

BUT THE HORROR WE SEE ON THE STREETS is only a sample of what is to come, says Dave. This is what America is becoming — more quickly than anyone dares to admit. This is the result of a selfish, greed-driven society that has taught its children to defy authority and do whatever feels good.

This is what happens when a godly nation turns away from the Lord.

So, what are you and I to do?

Weep?

Put on ashes and sackcloth?

Gather our children and flee to the hills?

Chapter 2

You Are the Light **of the Earth**

NO, WE ARE NOT TO RUN FOR SAFETY. We are to stay — as this great darkness descends on mankind. You are the light of the earth — set on a hill by the Creator You and I are to stay and live our lives in joy — bold witnesses of our magnificent and loving Father who loves us and holds us in His arms, protecting us from the turmoil and the terror.

We are not to run.

We are safe!

Our great Father will continue to protect us like a mighty fortress no matter what will be happening to the rest of humanity! And if we are killed obediently battling the forces of hell, then so much the better! Just think of what awaits us! Such reward!

Imagine the joy of arriving in heaven and being sur-rounded by an excited crowd welcoming you. As you look at their faces, you'll know it was worth it: the nutty little 9-year-old skateboarder across the street — there he is, filled with God's joy, rewarded for all eternity instead of burning in never-ending torment — because you kept inviting him to Sunday School despite his dirty little mouth!

And your boss at work — there the formerly pornography-obsessed, onetime-agnostic is in the heavenly choir, belting out a booming bass. Because you told him the truth.

And there's the baby-sitter that you learned was dabbling in Satanism. You spent long hours with her, praying that the evil bondage over her would be broken! There she is, excited, thanking you and telling John Wesley and Corrie ten Boom and the Apostle James that you were the one who led her to Jesus.

OH, THE WONDER OF ETERNITY in the exhilarating presence of our God who loves us so! He's been your friend for so long. You've depended on Him for everything. And, now, for the first time you'll really experience His presence — and it will be so overpowering, far more delightful and unending than any earthly pleasures that He gave you down here.

Suddenly, the Apostle Paul's puzzling words in Philippians 1:21 will make perfect sense: "For to me to live is Christ, and to die is gain." Yes, we have such a rewarding job to do down here when we obey and submit to God's plan for us — and if martyrdom results, well, we win!

No, we cannot run away from the dark days ahead.

We are to stay where we are — unless we hear the Lord clearly guiding us to a place of ministry elsewhere in the battle and turmoil.

RIGHT WHERE THE LORD HAS PLACED US, we are to continue depending on our great and wonderful God for our needs and wants and protection. The banks and bonds and stock markets are going to fail very soon.

But while mankind weeps, we will not be destitute.

Nor will we need guns to protect what is ours.

He is our Protector.

We will not need to be stingy with the food that we will have plenty of.

He is our Provider.

Nor will we be crying out for answers as the rest of the world seems to enter a new Dark Ages.

No, He will be our Guide.

He will bring us through the terrible times to come. We are not to run away to the seemingly safe mountains. Not unless we hear His voice telling us to go.

No, we're to stay.

"Nicky, " Dave told me, "I have been called as a minister of the Gospel, to minister here in New York City although I was perfectly content in Texas. Now no demon, no devil, hell or anybody else is going to chase me out. I am in New York City to die if necessary for Jesus.

"I want to tell you something, I don't have to love the city that is New York to preach in New York. You can't love a city that is full of murder and rape and incest — a city that is destroying its children.

"I'M NOT CALLED TO BRICK AND MORTAR — to save the Empire State Building or the World Trade Center or Rockefeller Center — no, we're called to the people of this hurting, decaying city. We are to love the people of New York.

"You don't love a city that's gone crazy. You love Jesus' hurting, lost children that fill this crumbling metropolis.

"It doesn't matter how much hell breaks loose, it doesn't matter if the foundations of the whole city collapse, we are going to be here preaching Jesus and pastoring and shepherding. Hallelujah! And I thank God there are a lot of people who feel the same way. They have no plans of running, no matter what happens. God help us, if we had a whole church of people who wanted to flee to the safety of Miami.

"I'll tell you what, you run and hide in Miami, and you'll find that the terror is not confined to New York City. All hell has broken loose down there, too — and it'll get worse wherever you run. Go down there or to Los Angeles or Chicago and you will wish you were back in New York — if that's where God has put you."

But if such dangerous times are ahead, won't it be terrible to have to stay behind in the chaos and horror?

"NICKY," DAVE TOLD ME, "the Word of God makes it very clear that God will do nothing in the way of judgment, until He warns his servants.

He warned all the people of Noah's time. Most scoffed ... and *drowned* — except for the eight servants, Noah and his immediate family.

He warned the people of Sodom and Gomorrah. They scoffed and *burned* — except for the servants, Lot and his family.

The Lord warned Jerusalem over and over. They rebelled and scoffed and *became slaves* — taken from their Promised Land and into bondage in Babylon and the far corners of the earth until Hitler's terrible Holocaust. Now, a remnant has returned to Judea, Samaria and Galilee.

And the Lord warned Nineveh. But they listened. An entire metropolis fell on its face in abject repentance. Even the cattle were draped in ashes and sackcloth as a sign of humility before the Lord.

The disaster was averted. God withheld His judgment. Can't that happen with New York — and America?

Of course, Dave says.

"But I believe the day has passed that it will."

Chapter 3

How New York **Will Fall**

SO, AS THE DARKNESS DESCENDS across the earth, what are we believers supposed to do?

Be faithful.

Obey.

Trust in a loving, protecting God who has promised that we will pass through the fire, but that it will not touch us.

Remember Daniel. This faithful young believer was hauled off to Babylon's equivalent of the "re-education camps" in today's Vietnam and China. He was a slave and a potential offering to a pagan god — if he did not cooperate. Instead, the Lord gave him boldness, power and brought him to the attention of the king himself, who raised him up in a place of honor.

God has done this so many times. Things may be going absolutely terribly, yet the faithful are protected —

read your Bible about Joseph, who rose from slave to Egypt's prime minister. Or Esther who went from captive harem girl to queen of all Persia.

What *is* going to happen to us?

IT'S ALREADY HAPPENING! Some economists are saying that America has been in a serious Depression for some time, but that the government juggles the figures to hold down the panic.

Look around you. It is almost impossible for a family to live on one income. That has not happened before in our history. Wives are having to leave their children with strangers and enter the work force.

But, more and more, Christians are hearing the Lord tell the wives to leave their jobs to nurture our important next generation — and that the Lord will provide.

Already believers in the Third World are living out the Book of Acts — depending on God for everything as their economies disintegrate. Just look at Argentina, once the breadbasket of South America. Now it's an economic disaster, complete with food riots. But believers are not starving. They are sharing, pooling what they have — and rejoicing amid the terror, just as the faithful behind what was the Iron Curtain have been doing for half a century ... and, unfortunately, as they will have to do again.

IN 1973, THE LORD TOLD DAVE that as the time of judgment came near, there would be a spiritual awakening behind the Iron and Bamboo Curtains. At the same time, Christians in the United States and other free countries would begin to come under insidious and subtle attack.

"While believers in free nations experience a wave of real persecution, the Iron and Bamboo Curtain countries will experience a short period of spiritual awakening.

Those who have lived under terrible religious persecution will enjoy a limited period of freedom. God's Holy Spirit will split the Iron and Bamboo Curtains and will seek out and find hungry hearts in Russia, China and Eastern Europe," Dave forecasted in 1973.

"God is bringing to pass a temporary truce between the East and the West for the express purpose of getting the Gospel into these Communist countries.

"Ironically, while the doors are beginning to close on our side of the Curtains, the doors will begin to open on the other side. And, after a short period of freedom and spiritual awakening among many, the doors will suddenly close, and the persecution madness will begin with intensity and engulf all nations."

REMEMBER THAT PROPHESY WAS MADE at the height of the Cold War, only six years after Soviet tanks trampled the "Prague Spring" uprising in Czechoslovakia.

Now, as Christians are coming under increasing criticism, disfavor and outright persecution in the West, as liberty sweeps through the Communist bloc, what are we to do to get ready for the worst-yet-to-come?

"When God called us to New York City," Dave said, "He told me to find a remnant, build that remnant into the image of Jesus and warn of judgments that are about to come fast and swift.

"Now it's time to warn."

IS DAVE A PROPHET? Is he the Jeremiah or Isaiah of our times? "I'm not a prophet," he told me. "I believe the Lord has raised me and others up as watchmen."

What is the role of watchmen? "Look at Ezekiel 33:1-9. It says if the watchman sees the trouble coming and he doesn't warn, the Lord will hold him responsible for the blood of the unwarned innocents.

"I want no blood on my hands, Nicky. I want to speak what the Lord has warned."

Then, what is coming?

"First of all, there is going to be a huge black hole of financial chaos in New York City's municipal budget. Already, they can't add any cops, they can't even fill a pot-hole on the street anymore."

I KNEW WHAT HE WAS SAYING. New York's publicly owned buildings and structures and utilities are falling apart. On TV a few nights ago, they showed how the bridges across the Hudson and East Rivers are in danger-ous disrepair. The concrete holding up the piers of one in particular is almost gone — all that remains in several places are the rusting, steel reinforcing rods.

But there's no money to fix the bridge. They can't repair the water system, either — once the best in the world. They can't maintain the city's heating steam tun-nels — which keep blowing up and killing people and spewing deadly asbestos dust into the subways. They can't maintain the public buildings. Just look at the condition of the public schools — never mind the lack of education going on inside.

"THE BEGGARS ARE A SIGN, NICKY," he told me. "Don't misunderstand me, I love the homeless. We constantly reach out to them. We are helping them. "

I know that Times Square Church has a heart for the street people. The services are filled with ragged people, sitting right next to businessmen in suits. The Times Square Church constantly reaches out — and has seen hundreds of lives turned around.

"We do everything we know how to do, Nicky," he said. "But there are 60,000 now on the street here in New York. When I was praying the other day, I said, 'Lord, I don't understand how this can be happening — particularly the millions now sleeping in the streets of Chicago, Miami, Houston, Los Angeles, San Francisco — a ragged army, itself beseiged by despair, poverty, drugs, alcohol, and AIDS. So many are mentally ill — just discarded by America.

"Why suddenly do we look out and there's this ragged army right in front of us? It's a sign, Nicky, a sign sent to get our attention."

I've seen it, I told Dave. In New York, if you pull your car up to an intersection, the beggars swarm up to your window, in dirty, tattered clothes and diseased faces, begging for a quarter — trying to put together a dollar or two for a vial of crack cocaine.

"DON'T JUDGE THEM TOO HARSHLY, NICKY," Dave cautioned me. "So many of them are hungry. The sad part is that so many won't spend the change you give them for food — they're so addicted to crack that they just rush out and buy another vial of momentary delight."

In some parts of New York now, beggars block the sidewalk , holding little signs begging for small change. Many are becoming increasingly belligerent, menacing and violent.

"It's just the beginning, Nicky," Dave told me. "Thousands are just teen-agers — just kids, some of them younger than teenagers. They are sleeping in the abandoned cars and the trucks and dilapidated rat-infested warehouses on 10th and 11th Avenue here.

"They found 115 of them one night in one of those old shelters, an old warehouse where they keep their trucks, 115 of them, most of them teen-agers. They sell their bodies for sex and on 11th Avenue between 34th and 40th Streets, you can get sex for 25 cents from teen-agers with AIDS. Twenty-five cents for perversion and death.

"NICKY, IT WAS NOTHING LIKE THIS even when you were wild and running with your bloodthirsty friends in the Mau Maus. It's so much worse. You look into these kids' eyes and their sunken faces and you see hell. Many are longing for death to escape the prison of drugs and perversion. Most of them are dying with AIDS, tuberculosis or pneumonia."

While some of the destitute are anxious to get off the street and eager to be helped, others are incredibly more difficult.

"One of our beggars made national headlines, Nicky. A bag lady not far from where we live attracted the attention of some lawyers from the American Civil Liberties Union. They took her under their wing, got her money and lots of publicity."

I remembered the case Dave was talking about. Actually, there have been several. The woman I remember was interviewed on national TV and gave testimony before various lawmakers. She was cited by the media as proof of our callous system's terrible abuses. She was given a job. She got a room and supposedly was beautifully rehabilitated.

But she left her new apartment and told the newspaper that she actually preferred to be on the streets.

"You go up there now, and she's on one of those subway grates where the heat comes up," Dave said.

The woman I'm thinking of curses everybody who goes by her steam vent. It's hard to believe that she's the same woman on TV who was so nicely dressed, well groomed and articulate. Is it an act? Is she insane? Is she doing research for her doctorate? Is she demon-possessed? I don't pretend to know.

"I TRIED TO HELP A BAG LADY RECENTLY," Dave told me. "I tried to get Welfare to get her a room. She said, 'David, leave me alone. I've had a room. I'm so used to being out, I don't want it. Leave me alone, please.'

"There are so many homeless," said Dave.

Silently, he shook his head.

I didn't say anything, either.

"God help us if we ignore their needs, Nicky," he said. "But I want to show you something. When judgment came upon Israel, Isaiah cried out, 'Thy sons have fainted, they lay at the head of all the streets.' If you read it as 'the intersection' rather than 'the head of … the street', it says: 'They lie at the intersections of all your streets as a wild bull in a net. They are full of the fury of the Lord, the rebuke of thy God.'"

"This seems to be a most prosperous hour in American history. Unemployment is supposedly the lowest it has ever been. Why, in a time of prosperity, do we have hundreds and hundreds — thousands — begging on the streets? The beggars are a sign, Nicky, an illustrated sermon of His judgment.

"This is just the beginning," Dave says.

Soon there will be panic and despair and anarchy as New York City loses the ability to maintain order.

"GOD SPOKE TO MY HEART and showed me that He is going to judge New York City by taking its tax base away," Dave said. "This morning, the *New York Times* said there are 6 million empty square feet of commercial space in New York City. That's 14 per cent of the office buildings — empty right now, not paying any taxes."

Think of your own household budget. If your house is falling apart, you can't clothe your kids and you can barely afford to keep your old clunker of a car running, what's going to happen if you have a 14 per cent drop in your income? The kids are just going to have to stay healthy and forget about college, right? No emergencies or frills will be possible. Maybe you can boost your lifestyle temporarily with VISA and MasterCard, but after you can't make the payments, you'll have to take bankruptcy.

Then nobody will lend you any more money. Like New York City, you'll just have to let the roof leak, put plywood over that broken-out window, let the rusty car sit and explain to the kids that there will be no more MacDonald's — much less designer tennis shoes.

"THERE'S GOING TO BE AN EXODUS of businesses out of this city," said Dave — who says that the Lord showed him the city will try to solve its budget woes by boosting taxes again.

But that won't work. A tax hike will just spur the mass departure of businesses already plaguing the city. Tax revenues will continue to plunge. As a result of the stock market's 1987 Black Monday alone, 37,000 jobs were lost — with the resulting loss of tax receipts by the city.

What will happen when there is simply no extra money? Will the city come to its senses and fall to its knees?

"I got to thinking," Dave told me. "If there is no money, that means that they can't give money to the abortion clinics. Maybe that's how the Lord is going to shut them down. Maybe they will cut off all that money going down to Greenwich Village where tax money supports pornographic art such as the cross of Jesus Christ dipped in urine."

BUT THE LORD SHOWED DAVE THAT fund cutoffs won't change any hearts.

"Even though they don't have tax money they are going to set up abortion clinics in houses, if they have to, do it with butcher knives." Indeed, a coalition of women's rights groups have begun distributing a video that shows how to perform do-it-yourself abortions — in the event that public funding is cut off or the U.S. Supreme Court acts to further restrict fetal genocide.

"And the depraved artists will start painting their porno outside on buildings," said Dave. "Loss of funding is not going to change their hearts. So, the Lord said to me, 'Don't rejoice. That's not the point.'

"No, God is going to cut off this city. It will become a pariah — an orphan.

"America will turn its back on New York City. *And then shall they grope at noonday, as the blind grope in darkness. They shall be spoiled and robbed, and no man shall come to the rescue. Everyone that goeth by shall be astonished and they will hiss at all the plagues.* New York City has been known for years as the in place to do business, not any more. God is going to take it away.

"He is going to isolate the city, Nicky. Broadway is going to go into a tailspin. Then, its bright lights are going to go dark. It is going to be something to behold.

"There is going to be massive unemployment. There is going to be no real estate market in New York."

No real estate market? How can this be, I asked him. Because you need buyers to have a market, he explained. No one will want New York real estate — except at giveaway prices.

What about the Japanese who have bought up such landmarks as Radio City Music Hall and so many of the finest hotels in Manhattan?

"THE JAPANESE WILL BE GOING HOME," said Dave. They are going to demolish our bond market and then pull out. The same thing that came over Japan during World War II will emerge again — a new kind of nationalism that will overcome even their spirit of greed.

"They won't care about America. Deuteronomy 28 makes that very clear. Strangers will devour your strength and after they are devoured, they will go home and hiss at you. Japan is going home, Nicky.

"Nicky, write this down: God is going to embarrass Wall Street and the whole greed machine. Here is how it is going to happen. I picture a fatalistic, lethargic madness. Wall Street is going to drift into a disaster on a cocaine high. We have a man attending Times Square Church regularly, a real man of God, a former vice president of one of the Wall Street firms.

"**HE WAS FIRED RECENTLY.** He told me, 'Brother Dave, I wouldn't play their dirty games. I wouldn't work under the table.' But he said more than that, 'I wouldn't snort cocaine with them.' He said only two men in his whole department are not on cocaine. Everybody, including the leaders, are all stoned, they're making their deals under the influence of coke. They don't care, it's other people's money. *'Eat, drink and be merry for tomorrow we are going to get canned,'* seems to be their attitude. *'We are going to get fired anyhow.'*

"**THE POLICE RAIDED ONE OF THE BARS** where Wall Street executives congregate and picked up 140 people.

"This vice president said, 'Brother Dave, those men sit at those telephones making those deals, stoned out of their minds.' Do you know why it's not going to be a panic? Because they are going to be stoned.

"How is it that the Japanese market can fall 15,000 points and not affect Wall Street? How is it they have ignored everything that is happening on the face of the earth that used to make Wall Street tremble and it doesn't tremble now? Because they are in the bathroom snorting another line of coke.

"It's the same thing as the handwriting on the wall. Remember Belshazzar and the night that Babylon fell? They were drinking out of the Jewish temple's sacred goblets. Suddenly, this big hand appeared, writing on the wall in an unknown language.

"DANIEL GAVE THE INTERPRETATION and you know what the king promised him in exchange for the interpretation? A high place of honor in the kingdom. Do you know what he really gave him? He gave him a one-night room, because it was all coming down. The king didn't give Daniel anything, Nicky."

I laughed — and I saw another parallel. Amid Israel's terrible defeat, God had protected and blessed the obedient Daniel. Despite the horror and madness of the population of Israel being dragged away into slavery and exile, the Lord gave faithful, prayerful Daniel favor. The pagan, drunken Babylonians liked him. And that last night of the Babylonian Empire, God gave Daniel new favor with the incoming invaders. Daniel was taken to the Median-Persian king and given a new rank of authority in his court.

DAVE REMINDED ME of how Babylon fell. "They were stoned out of their minds, Nicky. The enemy was at their gates and the Babylonians were inside drinking themselves into a stupor. They didn't even have watchmen at the gate.

"Nicky, it's the same here. Wall Street's dying. It's all going to the European Common Market. Brussels will be the center of the financial world, not New York.

"Wall Street is just going to fade away. We are going to become a third-class power in a very short time. We can't even dictate to Japan or Germany a thing because we owe them so much money."

So, what will happen to Christians?

"God Himself is going to be in our midst and be our refuge in this time of trouble, Nicky. If the devil is going to fight anybody, he's not going to fight you and me, he's going to fight Almighty God.

"You remember when the children of Israel, the Hebrew children, were thrown into fiery furnace? Where was God? He was not out in some distant galaxy. The king looked into the furnace and he said, 'I threw three men in, but I see four and one of them looks like the Son of God.'

"We're going into a fire, Nicky. There is going to be suffering. Some Christians are going to be unemployed, and yet God is going to see them through. And in their furnace, they're going to see Jesus like they've never seen Him before.

"Nicky, I want you to read Isaiah 31, *Woe to them that go down to Egypt for help; and stay on horses, and trust in chariots, because they are many; and in horsemen, because they are very strong; but they look not unto the Holy One of Israel, neither seek the Lord!* "

"NICKY, I THANK GOD FOR AMERICA. I thank God for New York. I thank God for our homes. But we are born in Zion. This is not our home. We Christians are foreigners, we are strangers, we are aliens, we are passing through. Our God says, 'I will never leave you, I will never forsake you, I'll go with you to the end of the world.'

"And He'll not let you starve. Not one of us who trusts in God is going to be down on 42nd Street sleeping in a cardboard box.

"God is going to come down and He is going to fight for us. Nobody is going to stick a knife in your back. Nobody is going to put a bullet in your heart, because God is going to fight our enemies.

"I intend by God's grace to walk these streets as safely as if I were in Heaven itself. I want to get on a subway or a bus, and I don't care if everybody on that subway is shooting and stabbing. I will have an island of safety because God is in that furnace with me. Hallelujah!

"NICKY, LOOK AT PSALM 121. Do you believe it? *I will lift up mine eyes unto the hills, from whence cometh my help. My help cometh from the Lord, which made heaven and earth.*

"The Lord is your provider — not any government, not the mayor or anybody else. The Lord is our keeper. Hallelujah! The Lord shall preserve our going out and our coming in, every subway, every bus. Hallelujah! The Lord will preserve you from all evil."

DAVE BEGAN TO TELL ME STORIES of how the Lord constantly protects His people in the war zones of New York. One lady from his church answered her door to a man with a gun who tried to rob her. She started prophesying, and praying — and she chased him out!

"One of our workers told me yesterday how she went into her apartment and had a funny feeling when she went into the bedroom. She began to pray. Suddenly, her front door slammed. There had been somebody in there, but off they went — and nothing was missing.

"Hallelujah! Nicky, even if the fires break out like they did during the riots years ago, God is going to have a people who so trust Him, so depend on Him, who are so confident of His keeping power that they will be untouched!"

Chapter 4

Ancient Nineveh Was the New York of Jonah's Day

"NINEVEH WAS THE CROWN JEWEL of a mighty empire, Nicky," Dave told me — just as New York has been America's pride for so long. "At the very height of Nineveh's power and prosperity. God raised up prophets to warn of impending judgments. God Himself described Nineveh as 'that great city...[whose] wickedness is come up before me' (Jonah 1:2). Nahum called it 'the bloody city...full of lies and robbery' (Nahum 3:1)."

Nineveh, like New York City, was made up of smaller boroughs or precincts, Dave explained to me. It spread some 30 miles in circumference and was protected by a 100-foot-high wall. The wall was wide enough for three chariots to run abreast on its roadway, and had 1,500 towers on it — each of them 250 feet tall.

"Nicky, in Jonah's day, Nineveh had 120,000 children under seven years old," Dave told me. "So its total population had to be more than 6,000,000. In Nahum's time, it had a large standing army, powerful and undefeated. War horses paraded in its streets. Chariots thundered along its boulevards. Nineveh was a great merchant city, a world trade center. Three-fourths of the known world was under the sway of its power and commerce."

UNDER JONAH'S HISTORIC PREACHING Nineveh exhibited a form of repentance — but this repentance was shallow and short-lived. Nineveh soon returned to its wicked ways, and God was quickly forgotten. The city's wickedness and immorality were exported all over the world, and Nineveh and the Assyrian Empire began to flaunt their bloodshed. Thus God became enraged.

The Spirit of God came upon the prophet Nahum, and he declared this: "God is jealous...and is furious; the Lord will take vengeance" (Nahum 1:2). Nahum saw that wicked society — drunk with pleasure, success and prosperity, full of pride, greed and violence, a people at ease while robbing and shedding blood — and he cried out, "Woe to Nineveh! God is going to bring judgment again!"

NAHUM'S PROPHECY CAME FORTH years after Jonah had been sent to proclaim judgment on the city. God had been slow to anger and patient in spite of their wickedness, bloodshed and godlessness. He remembered the short-lived repentance of their fathers under Jonah's preaching.

Nahum's prophecy was more than a dream or vision. Like Daniel and the other prophets, Nahum was a student of the Word. He had studied the history of God's dealings with wicked societies in the past, especially the great city of No-Amon (Thebes of Egypt).

NO-AMON WAS THE CAPITAL of the Egyptian empire during the imperial 18th to 20th dynasties. Treasures poured into No-Amon's coffers from all over the world. It was the city of the pharaohs. Temples to false gods lined its boulevards. Jeremiah prophesied that God would "execute judgments in No...and...cut off the multitude of No" (Ezek. 30:14,15).

No-Amon had been an impenetrable city, protected on all sides, "waters round about it, whose rampart was the sea, and her wall was from the sea" (Nahum 3:8). The city was very prosperous and had added power from satellite nations. "Ethiopia and Egypt were her strength...Put and Lubim were thy helpers" (Nahum 3:9). No-Amon had almost the size and population of Nineveh before that city was wiped out in divine judgment. With its palaces, expensive art, exotic furniture, pottery and fine clothes, No-Amon was the envy of nations. It boasted a huge army and a great stockpile of weapons.

ALL THOUGHT NO WOULD LIVE FOREVER. "Yet was she [No] carried away, she went into captivity: her young children also were dashed in pieces at the top of all the streets: and they cast lots for her honourable men, and all her great men were bound in chains" (Nahum 3:10). Nahum prophesied this based on God's historical dealings with wicked societies in the past. "Art thou better than populous No?" (Nahum 3:8). In other words, "What makes you believe God will judge all others for the things you are now doing but let you escape?"

"Nicky," said Dave, "God has every right to ask America the same question today. What is different about America from wicked Sodom? Are we better than Noah's generation? Or Lot's generation? Are we better than the wicked people of No-Amon? Are we more deserving than

Nineveh, which God wiped out? Considering all past evidence of God's fury, why should He spare us, since we are committing acts seven times worse than any of these wicked people?"

NAHUM'S WARNING TO NINEVEH is a warning to us also: "Thou also shalt be drunken: thou shalt be hid" (Nahum 3:11). America is drunken with lust, drugs, violence, evil sex — and intoxicated with success and prosperity. "Thou shalt be hid" means this country will become powerless, reduced to nothing, unable to act or to solve problems. Our mortal enemies will plunder us. Society will crumble under the weight of unsolvable problems.

Dave's words moved my heart.

I began to become convinced he was right.

Chapter 5

An
Outreach
On Times Square

I WAS STIRRED TO ANGRY TEARS as I roamed New York's streets in the next few days and stared at the sheer insanity of this once-great city:

• On street corners, wild, mad preachers proclaim a dead gospel of hate and condemnation — intimidating passersby with long passages of quoted, distorted Scripture with no meaning, no love, no witness.

• I saw a man crazily banging his head on the wall of a tenement as pedestrians did not seem to notice. Seeking the Lord, I was cautioned to leave him alone. I did.

• Pimps, prostitutes, crack dealers all boldly sold their goods in broad daylight in front of the gutted buildings as cops drove slowly by, their doors locked, their windows rolled up.

• Ragged, angry kids were living atop steam vents shared with babbling bag ladies and lurching old men who trundle their possessions around in grocery carts.

• **AS I WALKED DOWN THE SIDEWALK,** newsstand headlines proclaimed that an art group had received $10,000 in tax money for a New York City exhibition that included a transsexual Jesus with female breasts, a crown of thorns, eye makeup and women's clothing. In sneering quotes a spokesperson touted the right to practice homosexuality without using condoms, then declared: "At least in my ungoverned imagination I can ... douse [conservative U.S. Senator Jesse] Helms with a bucket of gasoline and set his putrid [obscenity] on fire or throw [anti-homosexual author, conservative Christian spokesman and U.S. Congressman] William Dannemeyer off the Empire State Building."

• In other headlines, in Washington, D.C., former New York City Mayor Ed Koch was pleading with Congress to help stop the city's slide into a new Dark Ages. The previous year, more than 1,850 New Yorkers were murdered — most of them in drug-related killings, he said. More than 56,000 were arrested for drug trafficking — 3,500 of them in or around 343 city schools. Only three per cent of those were students.

"WHAT THIS MEANS IS PAINFULLY CLEAR," an emotional Koch told the House of Representatives Select Committee on Narcotics Abuse and Control. "Adult drug dealers are congregating near our schools, trying to hook our children into lives of drug dependency. This will lead to truancy, crime, and ultimately the destruction of many more young lives.

"We are now losing a ... war," Koch declared, "one that promises to exact a price far higher than Vietnam did. We are in danger of losing our greatest resource: *our people.*"

"NICKY," DAVE EXCLAIMED TO ME that evening, "there are 10,000 people sleeping in the subways here and in the upper levels of Grand Central Station. You can get lost in there. On 10th Avenue, there's an old, tin barn where they keep the salt for the roads when it's icy. There are 125 kids who have AIDS sleeping in there. These kids come into the church — often just to get out of the cold or off of the street for a few minutes. Many are deeply into violent sex and masochism. A lot of them are transvestites and involved in things that you and I cannot even imagine."

One of the most energetic missions to help these victimized kids had recently come under an insidious and growing attack. You undoubtedly have read the newspaper stories about Covenant House's 30-year efforts to rescue, redeem and restore homeless kids who have turned to prostitution on the streets of New York. Now in the headlines, one of its most vocal leaders was attacked personally — forcing him to resign.

Satan does not fight fair.

He does not want anyone touching his evil kingdom — particularly an outreach like Covenant House that has effectively used the news media to show how perverted adult recruiters seduce and murder the runaways flocking to the big city.

WHO WOULD EVER HAVE THOUGHT it could get this bad?

"I remember first coming in to this city in 1958," Dave told me. "Thirty years ago, this city was terrifying, but it was comparatively quiet. Although things were very bad, it was peaceful compared to this. You could walk anywhere on the street. There were some people on the Upper West Side who didn't even lock their doors.

"Central Park was a peaceful place with very little crime. There were brutal teenage gangs who were into violent crime, but their gang fights mostly were isolated. They didn't bother the adults most of the time — they were fighting over their turf."

How did Dave hear the call to come back?

"WELL, ACTUALLY, NICKY, I NEVER LEFT," he answered, his eyes deeply pained, his face pensive. He had returned yearly for summer street rallies.

Although I don't always understand this complex man who led me to Christ and is personally responsible for turning my life around, I knew what he meant: he had moved away as the Lord led his ministry elsewhere, but his heart had remained here on these mean streets.

He didn't have to explain the longing in his soul for our wicked Nineveh on the Hudson River. As Dave and I sat inside his new Times Square Church — an unique outreach to the forgotten masses in the most callous section of Manhattan's glittery theater district — I knew what he meant.

He had never left.

"I have been coming up here every summer, even after I left the city to go to Texas," he said. I had been with him during some of those visits.

"Four years ago, I came back for a street rally," Dave told me. "I saw nine-, 10-, 11-year-old kids bombed on crack cocaine. I walked down 42nd Street in the middle of one of my street rallies. I went down there and they were selling crack. Len Bias, the famous basketball player had just died of a crack overdose and the pusher was yelling, 'Hey, I've got the stuff that killed Len.'"

That day, thousands of homosexuals were marching in the streets, denouncing conservative Catholic leader John Cardinal O'Connor, for his stand against sin — calling him a "fat cannibal" and a "creep in black skirts" while St. Patrick's Cathedral was reviled as "the house of walking swastikas on Fifth Avenue."

DAVE AND HIS WIFE, GWEN, walked the broken sidewalks and watched a 15-year-old boy go crazy, knocking out plate-glass windows and shooting a pistol. They saw the teen prostitutes with AIDS selling themselves for pocket change. They saw the rubble of a self-centered city gone mad.

"I went up to Eighth Avenue and wept like a baby," Dave told me. "I'd never seen craziness like that before.

"About 2 a.m., I couldn't sleep, so I went down into the Ticketron island right in the middle of Times Square, where they sell tickets to the Broadway shows." Around him was evidence of the decadence of a city that had forgotten any roots of decency or godliness.

THE HORROR OF THE GREAT EVIL gripping New York City chilled Dave's heart and soul. "I began to weep and I began to pray, 'God, You've got to raise up a testimony in this hellish place. It seems like the devil has set up New York City as his kingdom. This is the seat of Babylon.'"

Then Dave found himself praying:

"Oh, God, raise up a testimony here. Why can't there be a church right in the middle of this as a bright, hopeful testimony of what God can do?"

The answer was not what Wilkerson wanted to hear:

"AS I WAS PRAYING, the Holy Spirit said, *'Well, you know the city. You've been here, you do it.'*

"That shocked me because I was ready to retire. I've been in this city for more than 30 years. I was ready to go to Colorado to write books like you, Nicky, or go to Russia and the Eastern European countries to preach. It wasn't that I was weary, it was just that I had put in my time, with 30 years on the streets and drug addict centers all over the world that we had a part in establishing.

"Let some other young man do it," Dave prayed.

"But, Nicky, God just broke my heart," he told me. "I was told to raise up a remnant of the faithful remaining in New York City and to teach them Jesus Christ. I began for two nights to walk the streets and weep and pray that God bring someone else.

"Standing on Ticketron island right down the street here, just a few blocks, right in the middle of Times Square, I heard as clear as anything I have heard from God: *'Come to New York City, find a remnant, build that remnant into the image of Jesus. Get them ready for the Lord's coming and then warn of judgments that are about to come, that are going to come fast and swift. Before they come, I will warn you, I will tell you, and you must warn.'*

"And then I thought, if I am supposed to do it, how do I tell my wife? We had a beautiful home in Texas on a lake. We had moved our headquarters there. How do I tell her that we're going to move into the city? When I went back to the hotel, she had been praying.

GWEN WAS SITTING ON THE EDGE of the bed and said, "We're coming back to New York aren't we?"

Dave didn't have to say anything. The Lord had already told her.

That night, Dave went back to Ticketron island. As he was sitting in the dark, praying at about one o'clock in the morning, a man that Dave describes as "a guru-type person" came and sat right across from him and started chanting occult prayers.

Then the yogi began speaking to Dave in a strange voice, saying, "Look around you. These people don't need God, they're all saved, they're all fine."

Dave had never seen the man before. But he was moved by the boldness and depth of Satan's lie.

DAVE TOLD ME HOW, as he walked away from his confrontation with the guru, that his heart was chilled, but his spirit was invigorated.

He knew the encounter had not been accidental. The yogi was one of Satan's messengers — and had allowed Dave to hear for himself the bold lie that so many believe as fact.

These forgotten, lost people really assume that they are fine and that this is as good as their life can be — even as they sit in the squalor of Satan's worst.

The Lord used that demonized guru to awaken in Dave a love — a compassion — for the millions who have submitted to such lies.

And, Dave says, the incident proclaimed to him in a mighty way God's presence and power in even a Sodom and Gomorrah such as Times Square. Amid the filth, sin, dispair and decay, God is there, ready to snatch His beloved children back from the brink of Hell.

As he knelt in the awesome realization of God's might, Dave says that he felt something else, too: that the holy forces of Heaven were ready to break Satan's evil grip on the heartbeat of New York City.

"I WENT BACK TO TEXAS, Nicky, frightened," Dave told me. "I spent three months on my face. I just shut everything down and laid in my room, seeking God.

"God spoke to all of our hearts. 'Yes, that's the mandate,' we began to see. And we saw a church, here, in the middle of the city, full of people, walking in the image of Jesus.

It was at that time that the Lord made Dave a promise that if he would come to Times Square and do it His way, He would put the ministry in a beautiful building that "would take our breath away."

"It would be beyond belief," Dave remembers. "And He would fill it up with people."

AND THAT'S EXACTLY what happened. "The amazing thing," Dave told me, "is that since we've been obedient and returned to the streets, we've had people move from all over the United States and get jobs in New York City so they could be a part of this. They want to be a part of what He is doing here."

Of course, he told me, the vast majority comes from New York City and from New Jersey across the river. But over 50 nationalities worship in the church now.

"THE LORD ALSO PROMISED US that we would not have to worry about finances, that He, our great God, would supply the need." That was quite a promise since Dave knew that an auditorium would cost millions of dollars in Manhattan — where land sells by the square foot.

But God owns Manhattan Island.

"Nicky, the Lord gave us the flagship theater of Broadway — the beautiful Mark Hellinger Theatre. This is probably the most elegant auditorium in America and God has filled it up with hurting people. It has been the most incredible work of God I have ever seen. We have people who sleep in subways and we have some of the wealthiest in the city. The two purposes God sent us here for were to

raise up a remnant and to preach judgment to the city.
Judgment is coming to this city. He is raising up a pulpit
here to proclaim that judgment."

TODAY, IF YOU WALK DOWN Times Square, you will
see Broadway's beautiful old Mark Hellinger Theatre with
its enormous marquee proclaiming in great letters:
"Times Square Church." Inside, its vast stage can seat a
large choir. Under its beautiful, gilded, domed ceiling,
thousands of plush theater seats are lit by crystal chande-
liers. The scene takes your breath away.

Just as God promised.

Sitting in the majestic setting, I felt like a French
peasant who had just sent Louis XVI and Marie Antoinette
to the guillotine and, now, must decide what to do with
the empty palace.

IF DAVE IS EMBARRASSED by the luxury that his
church inherited when it took over the dark Broadway
theater, he does not show it. God provided this, he says.
The opulence came with the empty auditorium. Dave
shares the pastorate with his brother Don Wilkerson, who
ran the New York Teen Challenge drug abuse center for
years, and longtime friend and Bible teacher Bob Phillips.

"My son, Gary, also came with me," Dave told me.
"They all felt the same burden. My brother Don had been
here for years working on the streets and Pastor Phillips
preached on the streets and got the burden also. Bob is
one of the purest men I have ever met. "

They have witnessed God's might — and Satan's determination not to give up his evil stronghold. For example, soon after the church opened its doors, wild rumors
began to circulate, such as the preposterous lie that Dave
had divorced the beloved wife of his youth, Gwen.

HE TOLD ME HOW HE ATTENDED a meeting and sat with some people who didn't know him. They said, "You go to Times Square Church? Do you know Dave Wilkerson is divorced?" Well, Dave took the opportunity to introduce himself and testify quietly that he's only been married to one wife, Gwen, and has been happily wed to her since his youth.

"The opposition doesn't stop," Dave told me. "It's more intense now than when we first came."

But Wilkerson is not defeated, not at all — for God's blessings continue to pour over the Times Square Church in a mighty way.

Yet, this new ministry has changed Dave.

DAVE IS STILL THE FIERY, confrontative evangelist of the 1970s, yet is a kinder, gentler shepherd now — mellower, with the warm heart of a pastor.

The pain of his flock has touched his soul.

The tenderness of a pastor is unfolding in this fiery street preacher.

I watched as he explained to me this new, perhaps final mission. His blue, penetrating eyes have not dimmed. Nor has his fire or his intolerance for sin — particularly when flaunted by public Christians. But the muscles in his face are more relaxed. The intensity wanes as he works one-on-one with these people he loves — and who love him — as he feels their hurt and knows their pain.

His gentle, subtle sense of humor shows itself a bit more often now — even though he may not crack a smile after deadpanning a wry observation. His eye twinkles. The hint of a grin crosses his face. If nobody gets the joke, he may wince, but not comment.

AFTER AN EVENING ALTAR CALL, I watched incredulously as a disheveled man came up to Dave and whispered concerns that made little sense to me. Once, Wilkerson would have quickly dealt with the man, passed him off to an assistant, then hurried on to more important matters.

But as I tried not to stare, Dave listened empathetically, nodding, and offering counsel. Then he gripped the street-dweller's hand. Together, they prayed for God's wisdom and God's answer and God's touch.

Only the Holy Spirit can change such a fiery preacher as Dave Wilkerson into a shepherd.

Chapter 6

A
Changed
Man

"I'VE CHANGED," HE ADMITTED to me one afternoon as I sat amid the beauty of his gorgeous theater-church. "As an evangelist I would come into town for a day or two and then be gone. I wasn't involved with the problems of the people. Here, I'm involved with kids that are sleeping in subways and splintered families that don't know how they're going to survive.

"As a pastor, you get a whole new involvement with people. You begin to feel their pain."

Now, although Dave still preaches fire, brimstone and judgment, the message is different, too.

"I PREACHED A CORRECTIVE message about two weeks ago, from this platform right here. It was a very strong, corrective message. I was preaching judgment, I was preaching correction. At the end of it I was standing right about where you're seated right now and I fell on my face and laid there for 45 minutes after the service.

"I was so convicted by the Holy Spirit with a verse that we're not to call evil good, or good evil, but we are to describe the works according to Jeremiah. We are not to chastise the righteous. We are not to bless the wicked or encourage the wicked.

"I got to thinking, 'Lord, was I too hard on the righteous?' And God showed me that thin line, that the righteous must not be rebuked. They have to be corrected. You have to have that thin line there. You don't put the belt to an obedient child.

"BOY, THAT HIT ME SO HARD. I was ready to get up and apologize.

"I got up 45 minutes later, thinking everybody had left.

"But no one had left.

"In that 45 minutes, people had sat and waited before the Lord. They said they heard angels singing in this place. It was the most awesome experience I've ever had. The Holy Spirit revealed Himself in such a measure.

"Nicky, today He is trying to reach the holy, sanctified people that are not sitting, wasting their lives in pointless pursuits.

"He is reaching out to the people that are praying for their kids and to the faithful remnant that sees the lateness of the hour. I sense judgment right at the door — *in such an awesome way.*

"NICKY, ONE OF THE GREAT TRAGEDIES of this generation — and one of God's greatest griefs — is that so many Christians are not truly happy! They put on a big front: singing, clapping, smiling, praising. But lurking just beneath the surface is deep misery. The joy never lasts. They're lonely and sad.

"The lack of victory in Christ is appalling! So many are hot, then suddenly cold. They can't cope with fear. Depression runs over them like a steamroller. One week they are high, the next week low.

"There are Christian marriages also that run hot-and-cold. One day all is well with husband and wife; the next day they are miserable. Some days they can't even talk to one another. They think, 'Well, that's the way marriage is supposed to be. You can't expect to stay happy and loving all the time!' Wrong!"

I was touched by his words.

And I knew he was right.

PAUL WARNS OF CHRISTIANS who need to "recover themselves out of the snare of the devil, who are taken captive by him at his will" (2 Tim. 2:26). This describes many Christians perfectly. Satan moves in and out of their lives at his own will! They have no power or authority to stop him at their heart's door. He flaunts his hold over them: "You have no power of Christ in you to stop me! You are my captive. You will do as I tell you."

So many Christians are caught in a devilish snare. Paul said it is because they are opposing themselves (see 2 Timothy 2:25). They won't do what must be done to be delivered from the devil's trap.

To "oppose yourself" means that you have set yourself up to be trapped. You refuse God's way of deliverance and victory. You struggle against His way — and set up your own false "way of personal truth" — the lie of "Hey, whatever works for me." That's why you're ensnared!

SO MANY HAVE NOT KNOWN VICTORY in Christ. Satan places fear, loneliness, depression or lust upon them at any time he chooses. Is this what Christ died for? To raise up children who are under the power of the devil's will? Is this the Christian testimony to the world: "Give your heart to Jesus, but your will to the devil"? Never!

"You can blame your unhappiness on suffering poor health, being misunderstood, or having an uncaring mate, boss or friend," Dave told me. "In fact, you can blame it on anything you choose. But the truth is there is no excuse for a Christian to live as a slave to the devil.

"If the devil plays on your emotions and you are getting worse, not better; if your problems are getting bigger; if fear is rising, joy is dissipating, sadness is setting in — it means you are a captive to the enemy of your soul and are being manipulated by him!

"If this describes you, something very serious is wrong. You must recognize the trap you're in and seek to be released. You see, if you have been serving the Lord for more than a few months, you should be growing daily in the grace and knowledge of Jesus. Your spiritual victories should be sweet. You should be assured of His constant presence, changing from glory to glory into His likeness. By now Satan should be running from you!"

SO WHAT'S THE PROBLEM? Why have so many become captives?

"Those who walk with God are translated out of Satan's reach," Dave told me. "They are snatched out of his kingdom of darkness and into Christ's kingdom of light: 'Who hath delivered us from the power of darkness, and hath translated us into the kingdom of his dear Son' (Col. 1:13). We are translated right now out of the devil's snare and into the very heart of Jesus."

The Greek word for "translated" suggests that Christ personally comes and carries us away from the devil's power and set us in a heavenly place. But God only trans-

lates those who walk close to Him, like Enoch in the Old
Testament. Those who are held captive at Satan's will can
not be taken up and delivered from darkness.

"Translation out of the devil's dominion belongs to
those who walk intimately with the Lord," said Dave. "You
can claim to be saved and to love Him. You can tell the
world you belong to Him. You may even pray, weep over
Him and read His Word. But unless you walk every day
with Him, you will never change. You will fall deeper and
deeper into bondage."

WHAT DOES IT MEAN TO "WALK WITH GOD?"

"Enoch walked with God," according to Genesis 5:24. The
original Hebrew meaning for "walked" implies that Enoch
went up and down, in and out, to and fro, arm-in-arm,
continually conversing with God and growing.

Enoch learned to walk with God in the midst of a
wicked society on the verge of being destroyed by Noah's
flood. Yet he was an ordinary family man with all the same
problems and burdens we carry. He "begat sons and
daughters" (Gen. 5:22). He was no hermit hidden away in
a wilderness cave. He was involved in everyday life with a
wife, children, obligations, responsibilities.

He walked with God while raising a family and provid-
ing for them. There was no hiding to be holy for Enoch!

"He is an example for us today," Dave told me. "As all
the signs become so clear that the end is upon us, many
Christians are running for the hills to hide from the
mounting calamities. So-called prophets are telling people
to come to their safe, rural havens. Christian Jews are
being warned to get back to Israel to escape the financial
collapse anticipated in America.

"But Enoch proved that the greater testimony is to
walk with God in a place like Times Square, in the midst
of the storm — *no matter what!*"

I trembled at Dave's words.
Such boldness.

"I KNOW WHERE I WANT TO BE when things fall apart. When the financial market crashes, I want to go back to Wall Street — where I was during the last crash on October 19, 1987! I want to be there like a modern Enoch, walking and talking with God, without fear — at peace, fearless, a witness, preaching Jesus to a people whose world has collapsed.

"Jesus said, 'Go ye!' not 'Hide ye!'," proclaimed Dave — a twinkle in his penetrating, blue eyes. "Nicky, I want to be where the Holy Ghost is — and you can be sure He will be on the frontlines of the battle, calling the troubled and fearful to Himself.

"Enoch saw this world as ungodly. His own society was wicked, and as he looked down through all of history to the very last days, all he could say was, 'Ungodly! Ungodly! Ungodly!' Enoch prophesied of these days, saying, 'Behold, the Lord cometh with ten thousands of his saints, to execute judgment upon all, and to convince all that are ungodly among them of all their ungodly deeds which they have ungodly committed, and of all their hard speeches which ungodly sinners have spoken against him'"(Jude 14-15).

Dave's words shook me.

AND NOW I ASK YOU: Are you walking with the Lord? Then you must see the world as Enoch saw it: Ungodly and full of hard speeches against your God. How can you be a part of what is ungodly? How can you associate with those He is coming to judge? He is coming with ten thousands of His saints to judge a sinful, lost world.

Which side are you on?

"I am not condemning the beauty of nature and the good things God has created, Nicky," said Dave. "We should 'consider the lilies of the field' (Matt. 6:28). But if you are arm-in-arm with Jesus, talking with Him, listening to Him, then you will hate this ungodly world system. You will take His side against those who talk against Him. You will hear Him say, 'He that is a friend to the world is an enemy to Me' (see James 4:4).

Elijah and Enoch, two men that the Bible says God took into heaven without requiring them to die, had something in common: They were both haters of sin and cried out against it. They both walked so closely with God that they couldn't help sharing His hatred for ungodliness.

"The undeniable effect on all who walk with God is a growing hatred for sin," said Dave. "Not only hatred, but separation from it as well. If you still love this world and are at home with the ungodly — if you are a friend to those who curse Him — then you are not walking with God, and your salvation is a sham. You are not walking with the Lord but sitting on the fence, putting Him to open shame.

"The Bible says 'Enoch walked with God: and he was not; for God took him' (Gen. 5:24). We know from Hebrews that he did not taste death. But it also means something deeper than that: 'He was not' as defined in Genesis 5 also means 'he was not of this world.'

"IN HIS SPIRIT, IN HIS SENSES, Enoch was not a part of this wicked world. He was taken up in his spirit to a heavenly realm. Each day as he walked with the Lord he became less attached to the things below! Day by day, year by year, he was going up, heading home, getting closer to the glory. Like Paul, he died daily to this world."

At the same time, Enoch was not guilty of being "too heavenly minded and no earthly good."

Enoch undertook all his human responsibilities: He cared for his family. He worked. He ministered. Even so, none of the demands of this life could keep him from his walk with God.

"As mankind grew more ungodly all around him, as men changed into wild beasts full of lust, hardness and sensuality, Enoch became more and more like the One with whom he walked," said Dave. "That's such a great goal for you and me.

"You and I are changing. And by now, many Christians should have become very much like Jesus. But instead they've become hard and selfish. They should be growing in grace, completely satisfied in Him. But no — many are reverting, backsliding, going backward.

"Why? They don't walk with God. They seldom pray. They seldom dig into God's Word. Instead they brood and get hard. They pout and open themselves up to the devil's will. The point is that, unlike Enoch, they simply do not love Jesus enough to want to be with Him."

I've seen what Dave is talking about — as have you.

THAT IS WHY THERE IS SUCH CONFUSION, fear and unhappiness in so many Christian homes and lives. They have no walk with God and no desire to be shut in with Him. They don't pray anything through — they try to think it through. They don't stand on God's Word — they stand on their "rights"!

But throughout the Bible and all of history, those who walked with God became men and women of faith. If the Church is walking with God arm-in-arm daily, continually communing with our Lord, the result will be a people full of faith — true faith that pleases God.

"SOME PEOPLE CONDUCT FAITH SEMINARS," said
Dave. "They distribute faith tapes, quote faith Scriptures
— all trying to produce faith. And it is true, 'Faith cometh
by hearing, and hearing by the word of God' (Rom. 10:17).

"But Jesus is the Word. 'The letter killeth,' Scripture
says, and without intimacy with Jesus, the letter produces
a dead, selfish, demanding emotion that is not faith at all
— and God hates it.

"Faith comes by hearing His Word and walking close
to Him. Not by talking without walking! We should always
be 'looking unto Jesus the author and finisher of our faith'
(Heb.12:2).

THIS INTIMATE WALK WITH GOD is missing from the
Church today, said Dave. "Faith is really knowing who
God is. It is becoming familiar with His glory and majesty.
Those who know Him best, trust Him most.

"Show me a people walking closely with Him, hating
sin, becoming detached from this world and getting to
know His voice, and you'll see a people who won't need
much preaching and teaching about faith. You won't need
'10 steps' on what faith is and how to get it. True faith
comes out of the very heart of Jesus. And it will be His
very own faith — not ours — that grows within and
emerges from our hearts!

"Think of how Christians are squandering what they
call 'faith.' Theirs is all centered on self — their needs,
their wants. And they often get what they want, but it only
makes them more miserable. Where are the Enochs who
spend their faith believing to be translated out of the
devil's darkness and into the hands of God's dear Son?"

ALONE, I SAT in the ornate beauty of the Times Square
Church.

How long will Dave stay here?

He doesn't know. They rent the facility. Recently, a British producer tried to buy the place from the landlord because its enormous stage was perfect for a multimillion-dollar show that had been a smash hit in London.

Times Square Church would have had to move elsewhere.

But God intervened at the last minute and the deal fell through.

How long will the church be allowed to remain? Never doubt the power and might of our great God. And never try to second-guess His timing. We're not permitted to know some things.

Dave just knows that he is to preach the Word here and now. God will take care of tomorrow.

And as I looked around at the loveliness of this place, I knew that things really had not changed so much from that night so long ago when Dave rented another hall and invited all the gang members from my vicious neighborhood.

I remember....

Like it was yesterday, I remember the pretty girl who tried to sing, ignoring our taunts. I remember the laughter of the murderous guys.

I can still feel our slaphappy incredulity when the innocent preacher let me and my thieving Mau Maus take up the collection.

And I remember the incredible change that began that night when he led me to Jesus.

Dave had been obedient to God's clear instructions to hold an evangelistic meeting with the worst young killers in the city.

Dave had been prepared for that night. Just as he is for this new mission.

You see, Dave is no ordinary preacher.

He is not awed by mighty men — only the Almighty God. One Sunday, as Dave was walking with me from Times Square Church the one and a half blocks to my hotel, I saw him become very uncomfortable. You see, he doesn't like to hear people brag about themselves or drop names. But approaching us was a well-dressed church visitor who pumped his hand and dropped name after prestigious name — then began declaring the importance of her own ministry.

Dave turned away from the woman. As she sputtered in midsentence, he shook hands with a mumbling girl dressed in Salvation Army castaways.

Dave has experienced fame. And he knows its emptiness. He has had Christian acclaim — and has suffered under its fickle faithlessness.

HE HAS BEEN COMFORTABLE FINANCIALLY. In Texas he built a beautiful home with many luxuries — including an indoor swimming pool. But they never felt comfortable in that home, and one day walked away from it — uneasy amid such blatant luxury. Today he lives in a 900-square-foot apartment in New York City.

He is and always has been a very sensitive man. Too many material possessions trouble him. I've seen him give beautiful and expensive gifts away. He gave my daughters scholarships to college — a gift that, at first, I refused. But when I realized how much he cared about my girls, it touched me deeply. We were honored and embarrassed — but I did not want to refuse such a beautiful gesture.

To come to New York City, he sold his beautiful Texas ranch for 10 cents on the dollar to a large youth outreach and discipleship program. The beauty of Dave's generosity is that he has remained wam and giving to those in need.

He still holds great hopes — when many would be content to have accomplished just one tenth of the things that God has allowed Dave to do. But Dave's great dream is to do God's perfect will.

HE IS GENEROUS WITH HIS STAFF. He loves them very much and treats them well financially. I believe this is one of the reasons he has such a faithful crew that has stayed with him such a long time.

A remarkable thing, however, is that a number of them would stay with him even if he could not pay them a cent. They have found their place of ministry.

Dave is a fun-loving man. He likes playing football in the park with his crew. And he is not above silly pranks. I remember well an intimate forest walk I was enjoying with my beautiful bride, Gloria, shortly after we were wed.

City boy that I was, I did not know the ways of the woods, but in the evening twilight, my beloved and I strolled hand-in-hand down a forest path. I was terribly nervous — spooked by the great silence.

I was used to the hustle-bustle racket of the city.

Then, as I held Gloria's hand, I heard a noise that I did not recognize.

WHAT WAS THAT? Tough guy that I was, I could not let Gloria know that I was afraid, but ... well, I knew something was growling in the bushes.

A bear? Gloria became quite scared. We were city kids. The only bear I had ever seen was at the city zoo.

"Don't worry," I assured her, my voice tense. "I've got faith. But, let's run out of here." Invoking the blood of Jesus and proclaiming our belief that He would protect us, I grabbed her hand and we ran back to the house.

Everyone listened with wide eyes as we told of our close encounter with what must have been an immense grizzly or perhaps even an escaped Kodiak bear hungry for a young Puerto Rican couple.

Then, I saw Dave at the back of the room, grinning like a Cheshire cat.

He had been out on one of his walks, communing with the Lord — seeking the Father's will in the privacy of nature. When we came along giggling like the newlyweds that we were, he could not let the opportunity pass.

AND NOW, IN WHAT COULD HAVE BEEN his retirement, this incredible, colorful, joyful man has returned to the streets.

With his faithful wife at his side.

Gwen.

What a wonder she is.

Gwen Wilkerson — Dave's secret tower of strength. The mighty woman that only a few know.

Section II

The Girl
Who Loved
The Preacher Boy

Chapter 7

A
14-Year-Old
Preacher

GWEN WILKERSON REMEMBERS well her first child-hood impression of the intense 13-year-old boy visiting her church. "I first met him when his father came to try out as the pastor of my church in Turtle Creek, Pennsylvania," she told me.

It must have been young David's spirituality that she found so irresistible, because "it certainly wasn't his looks," she recounts in her beautiful book *In His Strength*. "To begin with, he was too skinny and his sandy hair was too unruly. Except for his startlingly blue eyes, there was nothing about his physical appearance that I found especially attractive. I'd never been interested in boys, but some inner voice, some quiet conviction born in me that day told me that the visiting Rev. Wilkerson's old-est son would one day be my husband."

THAT AFTERNOON, she confided to her grandmother her girlish secret:

"Grandma, come here a minute!" she called when, unexpectedly, she glimpsed him again — arriving for Sunday dinner next door at her aunt's house. "I felt a shiver of excitement run through me," she remembers. "'Hurry, Grandma! You'll miss him!'

"'Miss who, child? What's all the fuss about?'

"'Come over here. I want you to see this boy at Aunt Marion's.'

"'Oh, him! That one? That's Pastor Wilkerson's son, David, isn't it? What about him?'"

According to her book: "'Well, Grandma,' I sighed, trying my best to sound dramatic, 'someday I am going to marry him. That's my future husband!'"

"'My goodness, child! How old is he? You'd better not rush into it just yet. Your mother and father might have something to say, you know.'"

BUT IT WAS A CONVICTION that would not go away. From that day, pretty little Gwen "never really looked at another boy." Why was she drawn to the squeaky-voiced kid who wanted to be a preacher? Today Gwen smiles at the question. She tells of becoming a Christian at age six — and knowing exactly what she was undertaking. The bright first grader loved Jesus and she wanted to serve Him all her life.

And when the gangly young David Wilkerson stumbled into her life, a quiet, discerning voice told her that he was very different from other silly seventh graders.

"He had, from the first time I met him, a clear calling from God. Already, he knew he was set apart to be a preacher of the Gospel."

"My father, my grandfather, my great-grandfather, they were all preachers. I come from a long line of ministers," Dave remembers. "I started preaching about a year after we moved to Turtle Creek. I remember at age 12 and 13 praying for long hours. I would crawl under my bed and just weep as I felt the Spirit come upon me."

GWEN REMEMBERS FONDLY how the fervent youngster spent his spare time reading the Bible, writing sermons and, at age 14, preaching in nearby churches without a regular pastor.

"The intensity of his faith awed me, Nicky," she recalled — a faraway look in her eye.

In her very touching book, she wrote:

"My father didn't allow me to date until I was through high school. But since I could take part in all church-related group activities, Dave could be counted on to offer me a ride home from church events."

Even so, Gwen's father did not believe Dave would make a suitable son-in-law.

"IN SPITE OF DAVID'S OBVIOUS sobriety and his willingness to work hard," Gwen wrote, "my father considered him a poor prospect for marriage. Dad himself had arrived at success the hard way. He didn't feel that a country preacher would be as reliable a breadwinner as he had become and he didn't want me to settle for a lower standard of living."

However, the two kids became inseparable.

"Gradually," she wrote, "everyone, even David, began to think of us as a twosome. Whether this was the result of mutual attraction or of my persistence, I remain afraid to ask. But by the time we graduated from high school, he was as committed to a future which included me as I was

to him. We saw our relationship as part of God's plan for
our lives.

"SURPRISINGLY ENOUGH, Dad never forbade me to see
David — a fact that probably says more about the obvious
seriousness of my intentions than it does about any soft-
ening on my father's part. He must have known that he
could not change my mind, so sure was I that David was
'Mr. Right' for me. But that didn't stop Dad from trying.
He'd point out that David never had time to take me any
place, and that his courting left a lot to be desired — all of
which was true."

Young Wilkerson was no average teen — by his own
admission. "My mother was a praying woman," Dave remembers. "And I remember growing up hearing my
mother moaning and groaning with the Holy Spirit. I
heard her many times praying, 'Lord, if David ever turns
his back on You, I'd rather You kill him than he be lost.'

"I would come home from school," he recalls, "and
sometimes supper wasn't ready. Dad would say, 'You've
got to wait, Mom's got a burden.'

"And the burden was her children.

"SHE WAS PRAYING FOR US with enormous intensity.
I was raised in a very godly atmosphere. You know, I have
had drug addicts say, 'Well, how can you relate to me,
you've never been on drugs, you've been in a sheltered
home, and preaching all your life.' I'd say, 'Well, I do it the
same way a doctor relates to a cancer patient without
having cancer. He recognizes it, diagnoses it and heals
it.'"

The intensity of such a heavenly-minded beau did not
discourage Gwen, she says.

However, there was one summer when David was home from Bible college that Gwen decided it was time to build a fire under him.

"I ACCEPTED THE ONLY OTHER DATE I can recall having," Gwen wrote in her book. The other boy was "a polite, attentive, and moderately well-to-do young man whose only obvious drawback was that he wasn't David.

"Nevertheless, he had the built-in attribute of making David sit up and take notice. David *did,* I had decided, take our relationship a bit too much for granted.

"The night I had my date with this new beau, I saw David's green jalopy circling our block time and again. I really didn't enjoy the evening very much, but I did take a wicked delight in watching David fume."

They were engaged by Christmas.

Their simple country wedding was in June. What followed was a tender, innocent honeymoon in which two naive children of the Lord began to discover the private joys of a full life together.

Today, four children and eight grandchildren later, the legacy continues. All four Wilkerson kids — Debbie, Bonnie, Gary and Greg — are in ministry.

With a twinkle in his eye, Dave told me:

"I have two grandsons that I believe have the call of God on them ....

"I'm working on them now. "

Chapter 8

Watching
and
Waiting

GWEN HAS BEEN A SPIRITUAL MOM to me — particularly when I was the wild and notorious Nicky Cruz, a virtual orphan off the street.

I love Gwen dearly.

My real mother, a witch and demon-worshiper in rural Puerto Rico, rejected me at age eight. Denied her love, I had to fend for myself, alone, a vicious little boy without a mommy's love. My dad, a spiritualist healer/witchdoctor, was unable to show me his love. That caused him to put me on a plane to New York when I was just a youngster. On Brooklyn's mean streets, I turned my back on my family as I grew wild and intoxicated by the mad freedom, easy violence and the heady lusts of my new, dark Gotham.

BY THE TIME I MET GWEN, I was a young animal ... but a bit tamed by the grace of Jesus Christ. Dave had realized that my friend Israel and I had to get out of Brooklyn and away from the enormous temptations of our not-so-distant past. After all, I'd already been jumped once by a vengeful enemy determined to kill me now that I didn't carry a gun or knife.

Dave brought us home with him to rural Pennsylvania.

"You invited us into your home although you hadn't met us," I remembered recently as I sat with Gwen.

"Yes," she said with a wry smile. "But I had heard plenty about you, Nicky. Believe me."

We both chuckled.

ONE THING THAT STANDS OUT in my memory about that first evening was that they needed a babysitter. Dave suggested that Israel and I — two just-converted teen gang warlords straight off the blood-drenched streets — could watch the little Wilkersons.

"When we came to meet you for the first time, we had a tremendous experience," I recounted. "That was when Dave said that Israel and I should babysit your little girls. Do you remember your reaction to that?"

GWEN ARCHED HER EYEBROWS. "Well, Nicky, I thought it was the dumbest thing for Dave even to ask me if I thought it would be OK. After all —" She gave me a motherly, knowing glance. "If you remember, we had to go see someone who was very ill in our pastorate and Dave said, 'Well listen, Nicky and Israel can stay here with them. The girls will be fine.'"

She pretended to shudder. "I remember that I exclaimed: 'What?'

"Then, filled with a sudden, inexplicable peace, I said, 'No, Lord, that's fine.' We didn't say anything to you at that time about being afraid or anything, because I thought, 'Well let's go!'"

"You really felt brave or something?" I asked her.

"I WASN'T SURE if I could trust you, but —" Gwen gazed into my eyes, every bit my spiritual mom. "I felt at peace. In God's peace. *Somehow!*"

She had been pregnant with Gary when Dave felt the urgency to go talk to the teen killers he had seen in *Life* magazine.

"I was carrying Gary at that time and that was my biggest problem with Dave going to New York. I released Dave to go only through the grace of the Lord.

"I knew that God was going to use him in some way. I knew something new was going to happen, and yet in my young life, being married and Dave going to New York was a big step in a little country pastorate at that time.

"BUT PRAYING TOGETHER and knowing it was God's will at this time to do it, I released him. Only through the mercy of God that I could do that — with God taking care of me and my two girls."

She basically took over the task of pastoring while Dave kept coming and going from New York.

"Yes, we had been pastoring there for almost four years. We had been together all the time because this was our first pastorate. And so it was very, very difficult to be separated when he was going back and forth to New York on weekends, and taking Mondays and Tuesdays off as the church would release him to do that. Remember, this was a small, country church."

Did she feel lonely being away from him?

"Oh, yes, I had to take over the church while carrying Gary. I had to lead all the Wednesday evening services and be responsible for most of what happened on Sundays. We had some times when different preachers would come in on Sunday morning, but I took over the services and the full responsibility."

And she was nine-months pregnant.

"Yes, I was expecting my baby in July."

"I'M GLAD I DIDN'T KNOW what New York was like. I had no idea what he was going into — a jungle. True it was not nearly as bad as what is here today. Nicky, it is worse than ever before.

"But I didn't know where he was going. I know now it had to be the Lord. It had to be a miraculous sense of direction for Dave.

"I knew that God was going to use him in some way. I knew something new was going to happen."

Chapter 9

The
Incredible Joy of
Being There

GWEN HAS BEEN CALLED the Miracle Woman. In the 30 years that Dave has been in the public eye, she has gone through five major operations for different kinds of cancer. Did she ever think of giving up?

"That's a hard question to answer, Nicky. Right now, it's easy to answer the question, but when the cancer first struck me was in Staten Island, New York, when we first moved there.

"I had colon cancer. Dave had left on crusades and meetings the week before, he wasn't even with me for that surgery. I was able to go in. I went into the hospital and had the colon surgery. The pastor of the church where our family was attending at that time was able to be with us. My mother came up, of course, but Dave wasn't there.

Through the five surgeries, she never became resentful — particularly when Dave was gone, preaching.

"I never became bitter over it," she said. "I knew God and I said, 'Lord, whatever it takes, whatever I have to go through, it's for Your glory.' And, Nicky, I can say that honestly today, as I look back upon my life: my family, they're serving the Lord and they are married, Christian partners in the Lord."

THAT SOUNDS JUST A LITTLE too saint-like, I told her. Surely it was difficult — her in the hospital and Dave off being a national celebrity.

"At first it was a sacrifice," she admitted. "I thought, 'Boy, this is a sacrifice for me.' What I learned down the road — through what I had to go through — was obedience to Him, being obedient to whatever God has called me to do.

"GOD HAD CALLED BOTH OF US into ministry, but my part was being obedient to God. At the very first, when Teen Challenge started, when everything started going in New York, I asked the Lord, 'What part do I have in this ministry? What part will I have in this?'"

After all, she had small children — one of them newborn.

"'Lord,' I prayed, 'I have to take care of them. I can't be in Teen Challenge in the city. I can't do it.' But God showed me when I was praying. He said, 'Gwen, you be obedient to Me and minister to your children. When David comes home, you minister to him and God will take care of it.' And I've learned that the hard way, but God has brought me through that."

In all honesty, does she ever resent Dave being gone so much — almost half of their married life?

"I would say that half of our married life was traveling, crusades week after week, month after month on the road.

And, yes, I stayed home with the kids during much of it. As I said before, it's just the grace of God that has kept us."

Didn't she ever complain?

"THE DEVIL TRIED TO GET ME one time. It's in my book, *In His Strength,* and I became very jealous because I was sick. And I said that Dave was in the limelight and he was getting all the attention and here I am, lying on this bed, I'm sick, I can't do anything.

"I can remember being very, very, very envious about that. I could feel a wall coming between us and I can remember saying, 'Lord, I can't go on any further.' This was the only one time in my life that I can remember when this wall came between Dave and me because of his traveling.

"I said, 'Honey, can't you just stay home a couple times with me?' when I was in such pain. And he kept saying, 'No, Gwen, I have to go.'

"And I learned he had to go and do God's will."

Her children, now all grown, are — indeed — a testimony to her obedience. Each is a very devoted Christian.

"GARY IS VERY GENTLE-SPIRITED and tender. I don't know that it's me, it's through what I had learned through the years in helping my children to grow up to be godly children, to read the Word. I've read the Bible night after night to them when they were young, read stories with them and did everything I could. Of course, I spanked them a lot too. I mean, I couldn't wait for Dave to get home, so of course I had to spank them."

What did Dave do to make up for his long absences?

"Oh, he sent lots and lots of toys home. And that was all right."

Once Dave said that because of the call on his life, Gwen became the father, the mother, the strength and the spiritual anchor for the children.

How does she feel about that?

SHE SMILED AT ME IN SURPRISE when I asked her that. "That's quite an honor, Nicky. When did he say that about me? I'm very honored that he would say that about me, because I don't feel that I was the anchor behind it all. You know Dave, he's a strong man, strong father. But as I say, I had to raise them, I had to do it."

Did she ever feel neglected by Dave, or did she feel like she wasn't qualified to be his spouse after he became so famous?

"THAT WAS A PROBLEM. Dave was in the limelight of it all, but I wasn't well known and I'm no star at all. But our love for the Lord through the years kept us together. 'Divorce' is so common that it is just a word today. You know, you just say the word 'divorce' and that's it. Nobody thinks anything of a couple splitting up when they can't make it work. But Dave and I never considered it an option. We never brought the word 'divorce' up. We had our problems, Nicky. You can't go through life like we have for so many years without problems, and we did. But through them God has kept us."

Is Gwen Wilkerson happy with her life?

"Nicky, when God called us to New York this last time, I saw restlessness stirring in Dave's life again, just when we thought we were going to retire. We had a beautiful ranch in Texas, the kids were grown up. I thought, 'Finally we can just sit back and Dave can write more books, and I can travel with him finally.'

"**AND AS I SAW HIM** getting restless I just knew there was something happening to Dave again. I said to myself, 'I know Dave, I know him well. I can see it again.' So, I said, 'Dave, do you think this time we are really going back to New York?' And he looked at me surprised. He was shocked. He said, 'What do you mean?'

"I just smiled. 'I know we're going back,' I told him. As you know, he had been wrestling with how to ask me what I thought about going back to New York. So, it was just God again."

Is Gwen happy to be back in the big city?

"**YES. I TELL YOU,** I have never seen Dave more electrified than in what he is doing now, Nicky, working with our church in New York City's Times Square. It's just beautiful."

But is Gwen *happy?*

"**YES, I AM, NICKY.** And if I could just sit down with every young preacher's wife, Nicky, I'd tell her to be firmly behind her husband. To be the prayer warrior. To take care of their children. To minister to him when he needs ministering. To be there, either way, with children or husband. *Be there.*

"That's what I've tried to do — to be there for my kids, to be there for Dave. It's been hard, but I've always tried."

I asked Dave about that.

"I was going to write a book on how to raise children," he told me, laughing. "This was a number of years ago. I got all my children together, and said, 'I want you to tell me what we did right. You are all serving the Lord and I'm very proud of you and what Jesus has done for you.'

"I thought they would say, 'Well, Dad, it's been all those long talks you had with us.' When any of my children were having a problem I would pray about it and ask the Lord to reveal the root cause and I would go to them.

"We would sit down on the floor and open my Bible and we would sit in the room and I would tell them what the Holy Spirit had told me. And almost always it would hit the mark and there was always something from the Holy Spirit. It was good, too, because they knew I was concerned.

"So, I thought they would tell me it was all those talks I've had with them. But I was shocked when they said, almost in unison, 'Mom was always there when we came home from school. She was always there.'

David grinned at me, wryly. "They said nothing about my long talks. But I know it's true. One of the reasons they turned out like they have is because Gwen was always there for them. They came home from school and she was there. I was always gone, but they had that stability of Mother being there all the time.

"They would come home call, 'Mom,' and they would get their milk and cookies and go out and play. It was just that she was there.

"I think maybe that's why a lot of kids are messed up today. There's not that contact when they come home from school.

"They need Mom to be there."

Chapter 10

On
the
Road

DOES DAVE FEEL GUILTY about being gone so much of the time?

"I feel more guilty about it now in retrospect because I can't take back those years. I look at my children and I see the work of God accomplished. God has made it up to us. The past 10 years have been very good and are getting better. I think it's important how you finish out your days.

"I SAW A PICTURE RECENTLY of an evangelist being dragged out of a courtroom, weeping and in chains, and my heart went out to him, it just broke. My cry at that time was, 'Lord, I want to finish out my days growing more in Your love and being able to set more of an example.'

"I do thank God right now that at this time in my life, I feel that He is drawing me closer to Himself. I'm settled.

I know He's put me here in New York City. I feel I am right in His divine order. The Lord said, 'Focus right here. Don't worry about anybody else or any other place. You just stay right here.'

"I've had to turn away hundreds and hundreds of invitations overseas and here in the States. I have no desire to travel. I'm called to be here to minister to the flock."

BUT DOES HE FEEL BADLY for leaving Gwen alone so many times?

"My toughest time as a husband is probably looking back. I was gone so much. We had to raise so much money to keep the ministry going.

"Looking back I just can't even conceive how she did it with all the burdens she had to carry. My wife suffered so much with those operations for cancer.

"IT HURTS, IT REALLY HURTS. I think if I had it to do over again I would have spent less time traveling. I thank God for the time I did have with my children — quality time. I think they would admit to that. But the times I was not there, like when my children were born: Gwen had to go through that alone. I think I was there when only one child was born.

"I was with you, Nicky, when Gary was born. I was obeying God here on the streets in New York. Gwen never complained that I was not there. Sometimes she needed me in the hospitals, when she was very sick and I would be in the middle of a crusade that I couldn't cancel. I think the most difficult thing is to look back at all the suffering she had to go through alone.

"That really hurts.

"I THINK I COULD HAVE BEEN more patient. Our marriage did go through some very trying times. But over the years it became stronger and stronger because she had such a commitment to be there.

"She saw her ministry was to me."

Chapter 11

The
Pain of
Obedience

"LOOKING BACK I CAN'T CONCEIVE how Gwen endured it all," Dave told me.

And then, he confided that she isn't completely recovered even yet — despite the enormous personal strength that she seems to radiate.

Keep her in your prayers.

"Gwen is even now going through a deep physical test with tremendous weak spells. I saw her the other night cry herself to sleep for two hours. I was almost saying, 'Lord, is there ever a time when suffering ends?' I've never seen a woman suffer like she has. "

DURING ONE OF HER BOUTS with cancer, Gwen wound up in so much pain that she had to take a very strong and addictive pain killer, Demerol.

"She had to take it almost every three to four hours for almost eight months, and became highly habituated to it," Dave remembers. "One night, I came to her bed and saw her just so much in need for relief of pain that she had realized that she was addicted to Demerol.

"That's when I said, 'That's not fair, Lord. I gave my life to work with drug addicts and now I have an addicted wife.'

"SHE WAS APPALLED that this need was there. She's not a drug addict, it's just the pain and suffering. My attitude at that time was that I can't bear her suffering anymore. Let her have all the pain relief she needs and I think the doctors felt the same.

"But one night, our doctor, who was a dear friend, said, 'Dave, I can't do it anymore. I can't give her any more Demerol. She's habituated. I love you both too much and I can't do it.'

"GWEN AND I SPENT THREE DAYS in that room to kick it, just like any other soul going cold turkey. What it was, the Lord was letting us feel the pain of the people we ministered to. I felt for the first time the agony of what it was like for a drug addict to kick the habit. Gwen's so strong in the Lord, that she came out of it in three days and has had no problem since then."

But, Gwen, doesn't remember that as the toughest moment of her life.

"NICKY, THE TOUGHEST TIME was when I learned I had breast cancer," Gwen confided. "It's one thing to have cancer. But it's devastating when you feel you're taking part of your intimate self from even your husband; that's quite difficult. That was the most tearing part of my married life."

What about when she learned their daughter Debbie was diagnosed with cancer?

"That was hard. I found out she had colon cancer in the same, identical area that I'd had and she was only the tender age of 24. She had two little boys at that time. When it's yourself, it's OK, but when it's your child it's a lot different. It was devastating to me. I cried night and day. I said 'It can't be Debbie.'"

Debbie remembers well how hard the news hit the family: "I know Mom felt that because she'd had cancer that maybe it was her fault that I had cancer, too. My dad, he seemed to be crying out: "How much more, Lord? How much more can we take in our family? But through it all, He gave us the strength. My dad was there when I was in the hospital, feeding me from a little cup and with such a gentle spirit. That really brought me through a lot.

"IT WAS SO HARD ON MOM. She had been through it already. Now, to see her daughter like that, I think that was the hardest part of the hurt. You know, to feel so helpless.

"One night when my mom and I were both sick, Dad just broke down and wept. He knew it was an attack from the enemy and not God's judgment. I wasn't there that night when he preached, but I heard how he wept in the service and said, 'My wife is ill, my daughter is ill —' but he preached his heart out for the people that night.

"THROUGH ALL THE TRIALS, it seems like God has given him more and more strength. He could have given up and said, 'God, you're just doing all this to us,' and gotten bitter. But all the hurt that has gone on in our family has brought us closer to the Lord, really."

"They did surgery on Debbie," remembers Gwen, "and they took out as much cancer as they could and she had to have chemotherapy. We took her down to Houston, Texas, for that.

"Nicky, seeing your strong daughter go down to almost 85 pounds within a month and to see her lie there with this chemo, this poison, going into her system — I could hardly stand it.

"**WHEN I WOULD SEE HER,** it would just tear me apart. Dave was with me — I thank the dear Lord he was. She was deathly sick and the chemo was going in and the doctors said that was all they could give her because she was loosing weight so badly.

"They said to take her home, 'You have faith in God, keep praying.' That's what the doctors told us, keep praying. The chemo was so strong in her stomach it ate an ulcer. Within two weeks she was in another hospital. They had to open her up again and try to take as much as they could of what was causing her such pain. They sewed her up and said 'She's yours again. Keep praying for her.'"

Dave was hit hard by Debbie's illness. "When we found she had cancer in the same spot that her mother had it," he recalls, "I worried 'If she has it in the same spot, then she's going to go through the same four or five operations as her mother did.' Then, a doctor who examined her said, 'Well, you have two daughters and it's going to spread all through your family.' The reports were frightening."

THE CHEMOTHERAPY ate a hole in Debbie's stomach and she had to have a portion of it removed. Dave tells how it was hard to see a daughter go through it. It was hard on Gwen, he says. Gwen had guilt feelings that she had passed it down to her daughter.

"She was back in the hospital when Roger, her husband, called me," Gwen remembers, "he said, 'Mom, you've got to get here. The doctors said that she's really low.'

"I SAID TO ROGER — and I don't know why I said it — I said, 'Roger, I can't come yet.' I hung up the phone and fell to the floor, prostrate before the Lord in agony, groaning for my daughter. I said, 'Lord, are You going to take her? Don't take her.'

"And God spoke to me. He said, 'Gwen, did you not give Debbie to Me? Did you not dedicate her life to Me? Now do you trust Me?'

"It was very hard to take. I said, 'Lord, we give Debbie back to You.'

"The phone rang about a half hour later. It was Roger. And he said, 'Mom, Debbie is sitting up.'

"AND I JUST SHOUTED. I couldn't control myself. And he said, 'Mom, why didn't you come at that time? What happened, that's not like you!' And I said, 'Roger I couldn't, I had to be with the Lord, I had to be by myself.' And Roger said, 'Well come now, Mom, she's sitting up in bed.'

"I got there, Nicky, and she was drinking broth, clear broth, but it was broth. And from that day she improved steadily."

The truly beautiful part is that she recovered so steadily and so completely and soon was expecting a beautiful baby — which arrived without serious complication.

"God's been so good."

Section III

The Pain
and the Vision

Chapter 12

Preacher
Turned
Prophet

A PROPHET OF DOOM. That's what so many people have called David Wilkerson.

He went through some humiliating times from the mid-1970s and 1980s when many friends suddenly no longer wanted him in their pulpits.

Why? What happened?

"When *The Cross and the Switchblade* and *Run, Baby, Run* were so popular — selling millions of copies — and I was traveling the globe talking about your conversion, Nicky, and about our victories over drugs and gangs, no one bothered me," he remembers.

Honestly, Dave never needed the books for his popularity. He's an exceptional, anointed preacher with a tremendous sense of humor that can make you roll on the floor in laughter. But the public wants sensationalism so much of the time.

AND DAVE WAS IMMENSELY POPULAR — a Christian superstar — the subject of a smash movie and the two best-selling books that were even being used in the public schools. "Who was going to speak against a preacher who was working with drug addicts and alcoholics?" he asked me with a wry grin. "That's like denouncing the flag and apple pie."

"But when I wrote the book called *The Vision,* in 1973, that's when the roof caved in. I thought I had a lot of friends. I had been in their pulpits all over America."

All of a sudden, people were saying his message was all doom and gloom. Negativity. Discipline. His friends wanted to hear prosperity and victory. Suddenly, Dave was no longer invited to speak.

It was feared he might plow into his unpopular holiness and righteousness message — or denounce specific sin in their midst — rather than tickle the congregation's ears with tales of his *The Cross and the Switchblade* experiences.

Well, it was a valid concern.

TIME AND TIME AGAIN, I have been with Dave when I trembled under the enormous weight of his words. One time at a large church in Anaheim, California, he rebuked the audience over and over, talking about abuses you just shouldn't find in a church crowd.

Dave, I wanted to whisper, *hey, lighten up.* But on and on he went, decrying drug abuse and the terrible curses it was bringing on a selfish generation — and upon the next generation of kids watching their parents get high on every new recreational chemical that their underground designer druggists could cook up. *Dave,* I wanted to remind him, *listen, these are nice church folks. They don't do ecstacy and crack, man!*

But he was heavily under the anointing of the Holy Spirit. He preached, he lectured, he condemned, he chided and he wept as he talked about such taboo topics as masturbation, incest, and homosexual experimentation. *Dave, Dave,* I muttered to myself, *how are you going to give any kind of altar call after this?*

But I was wrong.

Dave alone had heard the urgent voice of the Lord stirring him to denounce horrible sins among the devout. When the altar was opened, the aisles filled. These good church people were in need of detoxification, deliverance and rededication!

Easy sin. Secret sin. Exciting sin.

But God was not fooled. Nor is He mocked. And in these days, He uses people like Dave Wilkerson to cry out against the creeping destruction and decadence in the pews of Laodicea.

Dave's is a message of reality, not an easy TV lie of the sweet bye-and-bye.

He believes in prosperity.

"DON'T FALL FOR THE LIE that God is protecting the sinners and cursing the innocent," Dave proclaimed one night. "That's what it looks like sometimes doesn't it?

"You obey God's laws and can't even pay your bills. But look at the crack-dealing 15-year-olds across the street! They're wearing $150 tennis shoes and $300 sunglasses, flashing diamond pinkie rings and satin warm-up jackets.

"Does that mean that God's not fair?

"No, you and I are protected. The flashy kid crack dealers and the pimps and pushers and hookers are under God's judgment. They live in terrible fear of violence and death — and worry that their glittering possessions will be taken from them at any moment.

"Well, look at the first verse of Psalm 37, *'Fret not thy-self because of evildoers, neither be thou envious against the workers of iniquity.'* Don't be jealous. Now, listen to me, please.

"A man who once attended Times Square Church who told me he was truly a born-again Christian and filled with the Spirit of God was sitting with me in a restaurant one day and he said, 'Brother Dave, I see these young people with all this money and I've seen them drive their cars, and I have to work so hard and sweat for every dollar I get. It makes me so mad I get red.'

"WELL, DON'T BE ENVIOUS. There are a lot of house-wives and other so-called sane, intelligent citizens who would push drugs if they wouldn't get caught. If they could just get the money. They say, 'I work so hard and these kids come along and they live like kings, it's not fair.'

"My Bible says in Psalm 37:16, *'A little that a righteous man hath is better than the riches of many wicked.'*

"They will be cut off in just a little while. The wicked will disappear. You'll look around and they will be gone.

"Hallelujah! Now, go to Psalm 37:23, 24, *'The steps of a good man are ordered by the Lord: and he delighteth in his way. Though he fall, he shall not be utterly cast down; for the Lord upholdeth him with his hand.'*"

That's true prosperity — not the popular bondage of materialism.

IS DAVE A PROPHET OF DOOM? "I've been getting weary of warning about the judgment on America," Dave told me. "I went to the Lord this week again, like I have on a number of occasions, and said, 'Lord, what's the use?'

"Nicky, so few listen anymore, even the righteous seem to get depressed from hearing of the warnings. So, why warn the people when they won't listen?"

"Also, Dave," I noted, "Even those who do accept the message get tired of being reminded of it."

"Right," chuckled Dave. "So there is a tendency just to be quiet, and say 'Lord, I've said enough.' Jeremiah was like that. He made up his mind one day that he was tired of the rejection and the mockery. He said, 'No more will I speak of violence and spoil or war and judgment.'

"He said, 'Lord, I go out and I warn the people about judgment, and all I get for it is reproach and mockery all the day long every day.'"

But even so, I noted, Jeremiah couldn't hold it in.

Dave nodded his agreement. "Jeremiah said, 'I said I'll not speak, but the Lord's word was in my heart as a burning fire, shut up in my bones and I could not shut up.' I'll tell you, Nicky, I have a fire burning in my bones and that's why I've gotta preach this message. God said to Ezekiel, 'Speak and tell them whether they are going to listen or not, tell them.'

"There is an end to God's endurance. People say, 'Oh, I've heard this message time and time again, and year after year, instead of getting worse, we get better, we're prospering more than ever before. Where is the sign of his judgment?' Well, Nicky, Jeremiah spent 23 years warning Judah and Jerusalem that destruction was coming, an enemy army was going to beseige Jerusalem, and there was going to be starvation He warned up and down, and everybody mocked. They said, 'We've heard that for 23 years.'"

TO UNDERSTAND WHAT DAVE Is talking about, read Jeremiah, Chapter 25, where the prophet Jeremiah wept to the people, "I have spoken unto you again and again, but you have not listened. And the Lord has sent to you all his servants, the prophets, again and again, but you have not listened nor inclined your ear to hear." Elsewhere in that same account, it tells how even Jeremiah began to doubt what the Lord had shown him.

He saw the people's prosperity and he saw everything going opposite to what he heard the Lord telling him to preach. So, what was the answer?

Why did the Lord withhold judgment for 23 years and let Jeremiah look like a crazy old fool or maybe just an over-zealous mystic?

The answer is the same as today:

God is always determined to warn his people, so much so that He sends his servants again and again, right up to the time of judgment.

God will allow his prophets, even a greatly loved servant such as David Wilkerson, to endure all kinds of abuse and mockery because of His mercy and His love for His people.

Just look at what's happening today.

ALL ACROSS AMERICA, PEOPLE ARE HEARING the same thing from the Lord. Dave is not the only one proclaiming these warnings.

And what is happening to our watchmen?

So often, they are shunned.

Nobody wants to hear such depressing stuff.

In Jeremiah's day, when he wouldn't quit proclaiming doom and defeat, they threw him in a dungeon. They beat him. The religious leaders and the political leaders ordered him not to utter another word of judgment.

They tried to shut him up.

The religious leaders didn't want to hear it.

The politicians didn't want to hear it.

The Bible says they even put him in a pit.

There are a great many people today — particularly ministers who refuse to preach anything but prosperity — who hate the message of judgment.

THEY WILL READ THIS BOOK FOR FIVE MINUTES and put it down and slam their fists and say "I don't want to hear it, I won't allow it in my church."

They hate it, they despise it.

Absolutely despise it.

And they despise those who preach it.

Why do I believe that Dave's message is worth listening to? Why would the Holy Spirit send a watchman like Dave to us and warn of coming judgment on America? I'll give you a number of reasons:

• **First of all, to prepare the saints** to endure and overcome when the difficult times come. "We've got to be prepared," Dave told me. "The Lord loves our people with such a deep love. He is warning us."

• **Second, to awaken** the half-hearted and those who are spiritually asleep. "There is a slumber all over the house of God," Dave proclaimed in a recent sermon. "What kind of thunder clap is it going to take to wake them up?"

• **Thirdly, to tear down** all the false hopes and false security being preached by false shepherds. "Do you know that the children of Israel thought that God would never destroy the Temple?" said Dave. "They thought if they lived in the shadow of the temple, they would be safe. Today we have cosmetic Christians who believe America is a special, protected nation — despite the fact that we sell more pornography and arms worldwide than any other nation. They believe America is something special to God, and we'll never be destroyed. Well, Nicky, the temple was destroyed. Brick after brick, it was torn down to the ground, it was wiped out. The city was wiped out.

"We have people who will be reading this book, Nicky, who don't want to hear anything negative. They've been told by preachers that we're not to do that — just think on everything that's positive."

Dave shook his head and paused.

"Like ostriches putting their heads in the sand?" I asked.

He smiled.

MANY PEOPLE HAVE CRITICIZED Dave's book that proclaimed judgment almost 20 years ago, *The Vision*. There's no point in claiming that it was Holy Scripture, or that it ought to be included in the Bible or that it was written under the same inspiration as Paul's Epistles. Regardless of what you have heard, this book from a humble man of prayer seeking God was amazingly accurate.

Dave was bold enough to declare what he had heard in his quiet times before the Lord. The book foresaw the rising homosexual rights movement, the attacks against Christian ministries, and the crushing inflation of the years that followed the release of the book — and was filled with Dave's heart-cry for holiness and righteousness in a church turning increasingly selfish and hungry for earthly wealth.

He also foresaw what is happening today — where Christians are increasingly the object of public ridicule. Just look at the TV news. Let's put a spokesman for lesbian rights in a debate with somebody like Jerry Falwell. Guess who is treated like a social leper? The person preaching sin or the person proclaiming God's word?

NO, THE PERSON STANDING UP FOR GOOD is treated like a stern schoolmarm wanting to rap America's knuckles with a ruler. And the person proclaiming evil is embraced as a spokesperson for human liberty and personal freedom.

Look what happened when Pat Robertson ran for president. His Christianity became a liability, a matter of sneering criticism. Did they call him "the genius behind the Family Channel," or "the founder of Regent University" or "the popular host of a daily news show with a Christian perspective?" Not on your life. They called him a *televangelist* — tarring his good name with the same dirty brush that they were using to blacken the names of Jimmy Swaggart and Jim Bakker.

Dave foresaw the fall of the Iron Curtain, and a time of incredible new religious freedom in the Soviet sphere of influence. But he also predicted that it would come just as America's freedoms were being curtailed.

PROPHETS OF DOOM OFTEN HIT THE TARGET — and that's why they make people mad. It was hard to be obedient to the Lord as the wrath of men grew, Dave admits: "Even now when I feel God wanting me to speak out against something, it stirs in me and I say, 'God, I can't do it anymore because nobody wants to listen. Let me say nice, sweet things, let me get up and just talk about Nicky and Israel and Sonny.'

So, Dave took a year off to seek the Lord.

He remembers. "I was on the way to a crusade, Nicky, to Florida. In those days I traveled with two big buses, a Mercedes truck and the whole business that goes with a road show. I was preaching to 10,000 people in crusades.

"One evening, someone handed me a book, *Christian in Complete Armour*, big, thick, old book with 1,200 pages. I threw it in back of my coach and said to myself, 'Who has time to read that? I don't have time.'

"We were going down the road and the Holy Spirit said to read it. I started reading and I didn't get 20 pages into that book before I was on my face before the Lord. I was on the bus floor weeping, because I realized I didn't know God like this man who'd been dead hundreds of years. And I saw that in the pulpit, I was preaching sympathy and excusing sin. I was giving comfort to the unrighteous.

"BY THE TIME I GOT to my meeting, I felt so empty, I felt so dry, I said, 'Here's a man whose been dead all these years and in 20 pages he revealed Jesus to me like I've never known Him all my life.' I said, 'What am I doing?' I was going the way some of these other ministries have gone — headstrong in my popularity and success. I could have fallen so hard. I know I would have.

"I felt the Lord saying to me 'You don't even know Me.'

"NICKY, IT SHOOK ME UP, 'You don't even begin to know Me,' the Lord kept speaking to my heart: 'You've been so busy preaching and doing things for Me.' You see that a lot of people have that idea that our obedience comes from ministry. No. I believe now that it comes out of intimacy with the Lord. If you're not in communion with Him, you can't be doing what God wants — and you can't do it His way.

"I asked the Lord what I was supposed to do. He said, 'You shut everything down and get to know Me. I want you to do nothing else.'

"I got a little hideaway in Arkansas, a little garage place. I just shut myself in and there God began to reveal the emptiness of my ministry.

"I began to see the emptiness in many of the television ministries. There's so much that's being done in Christiandom today that is of the flesh. And I was in the flesh.

"I WAS SHOWN THAT it's never enough to just say 'Well, the need is there so that represents the call. I see a need, so God must be calling me to do it.' That's not enough."

He came back invigorated and excited — and full of warning against the popular glitter Gospel and celebrity Christianity. It was a warning that a great many people did not want to hear.

The hardest part is that David Wilkerson is an evangelist and a pastor — he's a shepherd who deeply loves his flock — not a Jeremiah or a John the Baptist thundering about impending doom. Of course, he is also a bit of a Paul, when you consider his famous letters warning Christian friends in high places to change their ways.

Like Jesus and Paul did, Dave went aside to seek the presence of the Lord — to be taught by the Holy Spirit and to fall on his face before Almighty God in humility as he re-evaluated his life. That's something that all of us must do if we are to keep our faith fresh and our walk intimate with the Lord. We have to be willing to set aside everything and go meet with Him.

When Dave came back, he had wise words of warning.

"I CAME BACK AND started writing letters, saying it's all coming down," Dave remembers. "I wrote long prophetic warnings, and I did it out of love." Dave wrote to quite a number of top Christian figures — his friends, he thought.

One of his cautions was: *Go into the desert, just like Moses, Elijah and Paul did. Seek the Lord. Put everything down and listen for His voice. Go of your own free will— or else God will prepare for you a desert in which you will be forced to seek Him on your knees.*

And, it made a lot of them very angry. "I made some very strong statements about television and ministries that were in the flesh," says Dave. "Sometimes I may have been in the flesh, I don't know, I thought I was speaking what God was telling me."

In the face of such strong reaction, there was a real temptation to just shut up, Dave admits. "I always want in the pulpit to encourage people. So, when I have a burden to speak out against something, I find myself saying, 'God, nobody wants to hear that. Let me preach something nice.'

"AND IF I SHRUG OFF THE MESSAGE, the Holy Spirit will convict me so strongly that I can't sleep, I can't eat. It just burns. Nicky, you know what that's like, you get that something that says 'I have to preach this.' It finally comes to the place where you say 'If I don't, I'll die.'"

And then you don't worry about what anybody says or thinks.

No, says Dave: "You just obey the Lord."

Even so, rebukes from every side can offer enormous temptations to denounce your detractors even louder until they are shamed and silenced.

Except that is not how the Lord wants us to fight our battles.

"I HAD TO DECIDE that I would not fight back. I was making some strong statements about how we were being given a last chance to return to the Lord. Then I would hear some evangelist criticizing me and my message, and I thought I had to fight back.

"But now, I don't fight back. I don't answer."

Considering the ministries that have fallen, it should be obvious how important it is for Christians to walk closely to the Lord.

"I really don't even want to talk about it hurting me, Nicky," Dave said. "If you are involved in the needs of others, it diverts you from your own hurts, especially in this stage of my life. I'm so happy with what the Lord's doing with me here in Times Square.

"I am content, so I really don't think much about what somebody might have said or done. I know that I can stand before the judgment seat and answer to Him. "

"**NICKY, I'VE BEEN DRIVEN AWAY** from the kind of prophecy where you hear a preacher come to the pulpit, and say 'I had a dream last night, or I had a prophecy, or I had a vision last night,'" Dave told me. "I believe in dreams, and I believe in visions.

"But much of it's not anchored in the Word of God. And I tell you the truth, there have been times I have missed it so bad. I thought I had the mind of God, but I didn't have it anchored in the Word.

"Because of that, I have been driven to the Word of God to find a Bible principle for every prophetic utterance the Lord calls me to make.

"In fact, Nicky, when God spoke to me about what I was going to preach tonight, I told Him 'I can't preach that until You show me the Bible principle. Father, You take me to the Word, because I want it from Your heart, and from Your Word.'

"Nicky, if prophecy isn't anchored in the Word of God, you're going to be believing all kinds of foolishness. You're going to be tossed by every wind and wave of false doctrine and you're going to fall for all kinds of prophecies that sound good, that sound spectacular, but don't have an ounce of truth."

I WAS WITH DAVE the day that Evangelist Jimmy Swaggart fell. As the scandalous tales were detailed by a delighted press, I saw Dave's pain. "I told him to separate himself — to go to the desert," Dave whispered, his heart aching.

"I told him," He winced. "Well, now he will go."
And then Dave was silent.

Chapter 13

Walking
Away from
Battle

WHY DID GOD CHOOSE David Wilkerson to scold some of the greatest Christian leaders of our time?

Dave doesn't know.

"I think it was hardest because, really, I'm not a prophet. I've had people refer to me as a prophet, but I know I'm not a prophet. I'm an evangelist."

I watched him and saw the familiar pain in his eyes. After all the battles, is David Wilkerson a lonely man? I asked him: *What about those who think you are cold, that you don't allow people to get close to you, that you don't have close friends?*

He shrugged off the hard words.

"I was listening to a radio program once when they were discussing something I had said. I heard a pastor's voice say, 'We've known Dave Wilkerson for 25 years and we've never seen him smile.' And I thought, 'That man there is the saddest man I know. And I'm the most contented, happy man in America. I walk with my children and grandchildren and I truly enjoy living. I don't even know where my great joy comes from.'"

I nodded. David Wilkerson is, indeed, filled with the joy of the Lord. But, he can be somber. "Do you have a close friend?" I asked him. "A best friend?"

"I have several very close friends. My best friend is right here, my brother Don, who is co-pastor here. I admire him very deeply. I have two sons who, as they have grown up have become my good friends, too.

"I'D LIKE TO GO BE with my son Gary. He's in London founding a church and working with hurting Christians in Ireland, Romania and Poland. My son, Greg, is in ministry with me here. God told me when he was 11 years old, *'Don't worry about that boy, I've put the Spirit on him never to worry about.'* And that's what the Lord did.

"I've been a loner really most of my life," he admitted. "I have not felt the need for a lot of acceptance or friends. I have friends, but my father taught me to go to a secret prayer closet when I am deeply burdened — and I come out of it released. That has been a practice all my life, to go to the Lord and come out totally at peace, knowing that I am to do in His will."

What about prophets from God who speak into his life?

DAVE FROWNED. "Nicky, we've got thousands and thousands of self-acclaimed prophets today. We've got schools of prophets. I've had so many prophets come to this church and they come to me with some message from the Lord that just doesn't ring true to what the Bible says. When I won't listen to what they say, they pronounce curses on me.

"That's right! I've been cursed by some of these so-called prophets. I don't believe a man's a prophet if he curses people."

I could see his pain.

AND I WONDERED WHY so many seek to be prophets. The Bible is so demanding of prophets — particularly in the extreme judgment that God wields against false prophets who claim to speak in His name.

"Nicky, you know what my reaction has been to have all these people declaring in my face, 'Thus sayeth the Lord, thus sayeth the Lord'? I've been driven to the Word of God. And I don't proclaim anything anymore unless I can back it by the Word of God."

What does the Bible show Dave we are facing now?

"I am speaking out right now in my ministry about the death of the United States, the downfall of America. We have reached a point where Noah, Daniel and Moses began to pray the Lord would deliver their own souls.

"But people don't want to hear that sort of thing, Nicky!"

INDEED, SUCH A MESSAGE is no more popular now than in those ancient days.

"Nicky, look how God dealt with other societies who turned their backs on Him. America has passed the hour of grace. America has been turned over to the hour of judgment. There is no question in my mind about that. I do believe there is hope for the church. I'm very hopeful for the church, but as far as our society, we are under divine judgment.

"Go to the 28th chapter of Deuteronomy and you'll see everything that is happening to our Western civilization right now."

He told me of standing on Wall Street the day that the stock market suffered its worst crash in recent history some time ago.

"That was only a taste of what is to come," he told me — describing the hysterical, devastated young brokers and traders whose dream collapsed that dreaded day.

Their god of materialism had failed.

Their $2 million apartments and $60,000 BMWs and gold Rolex watches offered no hope now.

BUT, DAVE, I ASKED HIM, how can he really believe that everything is about to crash? After all, one of the most popular Christian movements today proclaims that we Christians will soon rule the earth.

He shook his head sadly. "What they teach flies right in the face of what the Bible clearly foretells. But —" Dave sighed, "I don't get involved in that battle anymore. God's not called me to argue. I'm called to pastor the Times Square Church — and I have plenty to keep me busy here without picking any fights with my Christian brothers in national pulpits."

Chapter 14

What the Bible Says About America's **Last Days**

"DAVE," I SAID, THUMBING THROUGH a newsletter from Times Square Church, "Some of the things you say about America are so hard."

I paused, not wishing to be critical. "People are so used to hearing that America is God's chosen nation. We've been blessed through the centuries. God has used us to protect Israel. Can it really be that such hard judgment is going to fall on the United States?

"Nicky," he said, "I don't believe America is His favorite any more than Europe, or any other country. We are going to be judged just the way they have been judged."

"But this is such a hard word, Dave."

"Yes, it's a heavy message. The first time that I preached it, I tried to soften it up. I tried even up to an hour before I came to church, but the Lord wouldn't let me. Nicky, America is dying! The country's wound is incurable. It is now in the final throes of a terminal disease. The great empire is crumbling!

"This country is headed the way of all fallen empires. The time that God warned us about in His Word has come — the "dread release," when even the prayers of godly saints for a doomed land no longer avail.

"GOD SAID, 'WHEN THE LAND SINNETH against me by trespassing grievously, then will I stretch out mine hand upon it...and will cut off man and beast from it: though these three men, Noah, Daniel, and Job, were in it, they should deliver but their own souls by their righteousness, saith the Lord God' (Ezek. 14:13,14)."

But, I reminded Dave, God never yet has destroyed a society or nation without ample warning. "Surely the Lord God will do nothing, but he revealeth his secret unto his servants the prophets" (Amos 3:7).

• God warned Abraham of the sudden destruction about to fall on Sodom: "And the Lord said, Shall I hide from Abraham that thing which I do?" (Gen. 18:17).

• He warned Noah, too, that He soon would destroy mankind with a flood: "Noah, being warned of God of things not seen as yet, moved with fear" (Heb. 11:7).

• God warned Samuel of the downfall of Eli's ministry and of the destruction of Shiloh: "And the Lord said to Samuel, Behold, I will do a thing in Israel, at which both the ears of every one that heareth it shall tingle" (1 Sam. 3:11).

• Jeremiah prophesied judgment upon Israel because "the Lord hath given me knowledge of it, and I know it: then thou showedst me their doings" (Jer. 11:18).

• God also revealed to Daniel what was to come: "Then was the secret revealed unto Daniel in a night vision" (Dan. 2:19).

IN EVERY AGE GOD HAS COMMUNICATED His warnings to the people in different ways. He spoke with Moses face-to-face, to Joshua through an angel and to the Old Testament prophets in visions and dreams.

"Nicky," said Dave, "today God is speaking again — loud and clear."

But we're all so tired of hearing gloom and doom.

"Yes, there are false prophets: crazy, immoral, half-mad, self-proclaimed seers who are also crying judgment," agreed Dave. "But these people are sent by Satan to discredit the true word of God-sent watchmen."

WHY HAS THERE BEEN no spontaneous revival? Why hasn't the church recognized the terrible sin in the land?

"Many American shepherds — or, ministers — have become so blind, lazy and sinful that God has had to call upon secular writers and artists to warn this nation it is dying!" Dave told me. "Nicky, hve you seen the prophetic cartoons in our newspapers lately? One depicts the Statue of Liberty standing with her head in her hands, weeping in shame! Another shows a bloody finger inscribing the prophetic writing on the wall: 'Anarchy.'

"Unlike the blind shepherds, these secularists see the grim reality that is now upon us. In New York City and other urban areas, cartoons portray crowds walking over corpses! Bulldozers are avalanched by mountains of white cocaine — and are unable to make a dent in them!

"In book after book, financial experts warn of the soon-coming economic crash. They have seen the handwriting on the wall, and they're frightened. One well-known financial adviser has cashed out in preparation for what is being anticipated as the world's worst depression."

Dave, I chided gently, *what qualifies you to begin predicting ruin and destruction? A lot of people just don't believe it.*

THE OLD TESTAMENT PROPHECIES of destruction were based on sound biblical deductions, Dave noted. The prophets were students of the revealed Word of God. They studied history. They saw patterns in societies. They became well-acquainted with God's mercy and His long-suffering endurance. And they were able to discern the trigger points of God's wrath — that is, when He had had enough!

"Nicky," Dave said, "Daniel was a student of the Word. He came to understand the captivity of Israel in Babylon by reading the writings of the previous prophets. From their prophecies he calculated the end of the captivity, the time the Messiah would come, how long He would live and when He would die. Here's what he said: 'I, Daniel, understood by books the number of the years, whereof the word of the Lord came to Jeremiah the prophet' (Dan. 9:2)."

DANIEL LISTED ALL THE TERRIBLE THINGS that were happening to God's people in his day. He compared it all with Deuteronomy 28 and concluded, "The curse is poured upon us, and the oath that is written in the law of Moses the servant of God, because we have sinned against him...As it is written in the laws of Moses, all this evil is come upon us...for we obeyed not his voice" (Dan. 9:11, 13,14).

You, too, can be a Daniel, Dave told me. "Any God-fearing, praying Christian can do as Daniel did. Nicky, compare to the Scriptures what we see happening right before our eyes, and you will know beyond any doubt that America is even now under the fury of God's curse for disobedience."

How will it end?

Dave winced.

"Only the Lord of the Harvest knows," he said softly. "But here are some signs that Daniel could not ignore — and which we cannot, either."

Dave pulled out a list that caused me to tremble. "Moses listed in Deuteronomy 28 all the signs of the curse, Nicky. We need to be reminded of these dreadful signs which 'shall come to pass, if thou will not hearken unto the voice of the Lord thy God, to observe to do all his commandments' (28:15).

1. A CURSE UPON OUR CITIES: "Cursed shalt thou be in the city, and cursed shalt thou be in the field" (28:16). "America's cities are doomed," said Dave. "Our own magazines have declared them to be Western 'Beiruts' or war zones. Crack is tearing them apart. New York City is becoming unlivable. A murder occurs every five hours, a crime every 20 seconds. Our cities are headed for anarchy, and there is no turning back. Now it's spreading even to our smallest towns."

2. A CURSE UPON OUR ECONOMY: "Cursed shall be thy basket and thy store" (28:17). "Nicky," he told me, "this refers to our Gross National Product, banking and reserves. A curse will fall upon it all, bringing confusion, fear and uncertainty. 'I (will break) the staff of your bread' (see Leviticus 26:26) — meaning widespread unemployment."

3. A CURSE UPON OUR FUTURES MARKET: "Cursed shall be the fruit of thy body, and the fruit of thy land, the

increase of thy kine [cattle], and the flocks of thy sheep"
(28:18). This curse will fall on our crops and cattle.

4. A CURSE ON OUR FOREIGN NEGOTIATIONS: This
curse will bring shame and embarrassment. "Cursed shalt
thou be when thou comest in, and cursed shalt thou be
when thou goes out. The Lord shall send upon thee cursing, vexation, and rebuke, in all that thou settest thine
hand unto for to do...because of the wickedness of thy
doing" (28:19,20). "U.S. foreign policy today is in complete
disarray!" said Dave. "Our negotiators come home
confused — upstaged by Russia, upstaged in China. We
appear befuddled before the whole world." Indeed, I had to
agree. It seems as if we can't even figure out who to talk to
anymore in South America as we fight the drug war or in
the Middle East as we try to muddle through the hostage
dilemma. In effect, our diplomats negotiate with sneering
spokesmen who lie and immediately break their word.

5. PLAGUES OF INCURABLE ILLNESSES: "The Lord
shall make the pestilence [sickness] cleave unto
thee...with a consumption, and with a fever, and with an
inflammation" (28:21,22). "The Lord will smite thee with
the botch of Egypt...and with the scab...whereof thou
canst not be healed. The Lord shall smite thee with madness, and blindness, and astonishment [panic] of heart
(28:27,28). "The Lord shall smite thee...with a sore botch
[boil] that cannot be healed, from the sole of thy foot unto
the top of thy head" (28:35). "The mark of AIDS is the
purple blotch — the incurable boil!" said Dave.

6. DUST BOWLS AND AREAS OF DROUGHT: "The
Lord shall make the rain of thy land powder and dust:
from heaven shall it come down upon thee" (28:24). This
is God's doing. All of it is sent from heaven!

7. INSIGNIFICANT ENEMIES WILL SHAME OUR ARMIES: "The Lord shall cause thee to be smitten before thine enemies: thou shalt go out one way against them, and flee seven ways before them...And thy carcase shall be meat unto all fowls of the air" (28:25,26). Think of the stalemate in Korea. Or our troops fleeing from Vietnam and being chased out of Lebanon. Or shadowy drug lords in Colombia and Burma holding a gun to our head.

8. AN EPIDEMIC OF DIVORCE: An epidemic of broken homes has erupted. "Thou shalt betroth a wife, and another man shall lie with her: thou shalt build an house, and thou shalt not dwell therein: thou shalt plant a vineyard, and shalt not gather the grapes thereof" (28:30).

9. A WAVE OF BANKRUPTCIES: "Thine ox shall be slain before thine eyes...thine ass shall be violently taken away from before thy face, and shall not be restored to thee: thy sheep shall be given unto thine enemies, and thou shalt have none to rescue them" (28:31). This describes the ancient Oriental custom of the creditor taking everything from the debtor for restitution. It warns of the wave of bankruptcies that will come upon this cursed nation.

10. THE LOSS OF A GENERATION OF YOUTH: "Thy sons and thy daughters shall be given unto another people, and thine eyes shall look, and fail with longing for them" (28:32). Today a nation of adults, supplied with all money and might, can merely stand by and watch in horror as drugs and violence swallow up an entire population of youth. This Scripture is a prophetic warning about the despair that falls upon parents in a nation under the curse. "Thou shalt beget sons and daughters, but thou

shalt not enjoy them; for they shall go into captivity"
(28:41).

**11. PROSPERITY OF OTHER NATIONS AT OUR EX-
PENSE:** "The stranger that is within thee shall get up
above thee very high; and thou shalt come down very low"
(28:43). Hosea describes the blindness of people under
this curse: "Strangers have devoured his strength, and he
knoweth it not: yea, gray hairs are here and there upon
him, yet he knoweth not" (Hos. 7:9). Whatever the crop,
whatever the fruit, "the strangers shall swallow it up"
(Hos. 8:7).

**12. YOU WILL BECOME A DEBTOR NATION —
RATHER THAN A LENDER:** "He shall lend to thee, and
thou shalt not lend to him: he shall be the head, and thou
shalt be the tail" (28:44). "In the last five years we have
become the world's biggest debtor nation," Dave noted.
"At this moment we are now the tail — and Japan is the
head. We can't even bail out our own bankrupt savings
and loan institutions. Consider the $150 billion that's
needed to save our banking system — and then tell me
America is not under the curse! We are not experiencing
the full fury of it!

"Up to now America has stumbled along, enduring but
never solving its problems. Yet we have survived. But now,
all our problems are going to accelerate. "

Just look around and you'll see that Dave is on track:

• **THE HOSPITAL SYSTEM** in our cities has become
unmanageable: addicts are slipping out of their rooms,
running out to get crack, and then climbing back into
bed. Many are freebasing cocaine in hospital rooms —
even in emergency rooms. Doctors and nurses are being

beaten and murdered. There is no cure, no solution possible!

• **OUR JAILS ARE OVERFLOWING,** resulting in the release of many criminals. We are now building prison barges in the attempt to cope with the overcrowding. Our penal institutions are horror houses of rape, violence and hopelessness. Here, too, there are no solutions, no cures in sight.

• **OUR COURTS CAN'T HANDLE THE CASELOADS** anymore. Judge after judge has issued warnings: "We're on the brink of anarchy. We can't even process the multitudes of criminals."

• **OUR SCHOOLS ARE THE SHAME** of the whole world. Inner-city school buildings are decaying; teachers live in fear. The schools have become a miniature hell where kids are confronted with guns, knives, drugs, satanism, violence and promiscuous sex. The schools are devoid of all morality.

• **OUR WELFARE SYSTEMS ARE IN CHAOS.** New York State has called this city a "welfare basket case." Costs already have spun out of control.

• **OUR ECONOMY IS IN ITS DEATH THROES.** Nobody in the U.S. government, in Congress, on Wall Street or at the Federal Reserve can tell us what is happening. It is beyond us all. No one knows what is holding the system together.

"NICKY, THERE IS A TRIGGER that set off this awesome judgment," Dave told me. When America began blotting out its Christian heritage and defying the God who gave us all that we have, our Lord turned His fury against this nation.

"God must pour out His fury when the nation turns from simply ignoring God to deliberately plotting against Him," said Dave.

Just look at America in recent years.

As a nation, we no longer care about what is right. But it's worse than that. It's as if our nation is determined to flaunt what is wrong.

• **ON TV,** the criterion is "whatever sells." If it's a sneering, soft-porn package of greed and lust, then that's what is piped into millions of homes, twisting young minds and hardening adult hearts.

• **IN THE RECORD INDUSTRY,** if it's satanism and violent sex that our kids will pay for, then that's what is churned out by an industry with no conscience, consumed only with making a fast buck.

• **IN THE ART WORLD,** we are deluged with an ugly new defiance — obscenities directed at all that is sacred: crucifixes bottled in urine, paintings of Jesus as a transsexual — federally funded homoerotic photo exhibits of children touted in the national press as a wonderful expression of our First Amendment rights.

• **IN OUR COURTS, JUDGES ARE BLOTTING OUT** any remaining signs that we were once a Christian nation, ordering the removal of crosses, nativity scenes and biblical mottos from public buildings and parks. As I write this, new legal battles are being mounted against the city of Fort Lauderdale, Florida, which has refused to remove the tablets of the Ten Commandments from a World War

II monument and against the federal government to remove statutes of Jesus from two parks.

• **THE QUIET BATTLE AGAINST PRAYER** has moved into the last bastions of local determination — the little, rural, school districts now are being forced to give up Bible studies and are stopping local clergy from praying on loudspeakers before sports events. Our judiciary protects baby-killers and atheistic rights. Our judges shake their fist at God, daring Him to react to their flaunted rebellion. This small handful of wicked counselors has set their hearts against God. They have declared war, and God no longer can hold back His fury.

"I DO NOT CARE A BIT what the Supreme Court does," Dave told me. "You see, God is going to turn it into a kangaroo court of fools. These wicked counselors will go down in judgment. God has promised to confound them and to make their faces dark with fear."

Nahum asks, "Who can stand before his indignation? and who can abide[endure] in the fierceness of his anger?" (Nahum 1:6). When God's fury is on the land, when the fierceness of God's anger strikes, what judge can then stand in rebellion? What court will endure? God will smite them all with fear, striking their hearts with confusion. They will be helpless against the flood, crying, "What has happened? It's all going down!"

LIKE NINEVEH, America has an incurable wound. Other than a miracle of mercy, there is no more healing for us, only judgment (see Nahum 3:19). These judgments appear and quickly accelerate until each becomes an avalanche, an overwhelming flood (1:8).

What is on the horizon?

The following four points are straight from one of the Times Square Church newsletters:

1. THERE SHALL BE NO END OF CORPSES. The first judgment is that there will be "no end of corpses." Nahum 3:3 says, "There is a multitude of slain, and a great number of carcases; and there is none end of their corpses; they stumble upon their corpses."

Nahum saw something that at the time seemed unbelievable. Nineveh was lounging comfortably in its prosperity. Its streets bustled with shoppers and merchants — business as usual. But the prophet saw a sword coming to those busy streets. He saw corpses lying everywhere, a multitude of the slain and murdered with people stumbling over the bodies. When judgment comes, expect to see caskets and corpses in growing numbers.

A terrible scene is emblazoned on my mind: that of former President Reagan and his wife weeping over the 250 caskets of soldiers who were blown up in Lebanon. And again I see them standing before empty caskets — those of six astronauts and one schoolteacher blown out of the sky. I see President Bush, too, standing gravely before some 35 caskets — those of sailors killed by a shipboard gun explosion. It's coffin time in America! In the days ahead there will be so many corpses that Americans will become immune to it all — and will just step over bodies. One day we will see bodies dead from starvation on America's streets. Already AIDS victims are languishing on the streets with no place to die!

THIS STORY APPEARED in the news recently: a 14-year-old mother threw her newborn baby out of a fourth-floor window. The little child's corpse was found three days later in the alley. People thought it was a discarded baby doll.

Another equally gruesome story is that of a three-day-old baby found in a dumpster on Ninth Avenue, wrapped in a plastic bag — just one of hundreds of little abandoned corpses found in the city.

But perhaps the most disturbing story to appear recently was that of the tiny corpse of a little girl who had been placed in a suitcase and burned to death. The story read, "She was abused and abandoned in life, but adopted and loved in death. She was a toddler, about three years old, found burned to death in a suitcase dumped amid piles of trash in the vestibule of an apartment house.

"The body was going to be buried in Potter's Field, but the firefighters who found her were so broken by what they saw that they arranged to have her buried — 'to give this baby some type of dignity in death — she probably didn't have much dignity in life'... Trucks from the engine and ladder companies stood outside the church as (they) carefully cradled the tiny white casket in their arms and carried it into the church."

You can almost hear the frightful cry: "Come, all ye gravediggers! Come, all ye coffin makers, labor around the clock.

"Come, ye pallbearers, the caskets keep coming! Come, ye funeral directors and embalmers, your work has just begun!" There is no end to the corpses!

What kind of spiritual blindness has fallen on us when we see this judgment all about and still have preachers crying, "Peace! Prosperity!" Do they not care? Does it mean nothing to them?

2. LOSS OF NATIONAL PURPOSE: *"I will shew the nations thy nakedness, and the kingdoms thy shame" (Nahum 3:5). The second judgment we'll see is that*

*nations which once feared us, envied us and stood in awe
of us will discover us to have become weak. "Behold, thy
people in the midst of thee are women" (3:13). In other
words, "You have grown soft and effeminate through your
luxury. You have no will, no resolve."*

*All dying empires become soft and effeminate, unwill-
ing in the end to take a stand for anything. From Sodom
to Babylon, dying empires have gone out drunk, lazy,
stoned and immune to all warnings. Like Belshazzar, the
king of Babylon who saw the writing on the wall, they
end up giving the prophets their day in court — telling
them, yes, they are on target, that what they're saying is
all true. But then they go right back to the party (see
Daniel 5).*

*"The gates of thy land shall be set wide open unto
thine enemies" (Nahum 3:13). Drug lords from Cambodia,
Colombia, Mexico and Pakistan all are laughing at our
flimsy border patrols. God has torn down all our walls.
Castro has dumped hundreds of prisoners and spies on
our land.*

*Thank God for the many good — even godly — aliens
I've met. But for every good one, 10 evil ones, including
murderers and rapists, pour in. In many countries drug
pushers are the only ones able to raise the money to
come to America. The prophet said they came with a
sword to kill and destroy.*

3. A BAPTISM OF FILTH *"I will cast abominable filth
upon thee, and make thee vile, and will set thee as a
gazingstock" (3:6). Our third judgment, like Nineveh, is
that we have become the shame and disgrace of the
world. The rest of the world blushes at our wickedness. I
once took visitors from Poland and other Soviet-bloc
countries on a tour through New York's streets. As we
walked down 42nd Street, I saw tears in their eyes. Fi-*

nally, one Polish businessman turned to me and said, "I'm walking through hell itself! Please take me out of here!"

"This is the rejoicing city that dwelt carelessly, that said in her heart, I am, and there is none beside me: how is she become a desolation, a place for beasts to lie down in! every one that passeth by her shall hiss, and wag his hand" (Zeph. 2:15). Israel once became so wicked that even the heathen "daughters of the Philistines...are ashamed of thy lewd way" (Ezek. 16:27). Israel's corruption was worse than Sodom's. "Thou wast corrupted more than they in all thy ways" (Ezek. 16:47).

Moses warned Israel that sin would bring any nation "into desolation: and your enemies which dwell therein shall be astonished at it" (Lev. 26:32).

America is now experiencing this supernatural baptism of filth. The prophet paints the picture of a God so furious, so full of vengeance, that He is throwing mud or dirt on this wicked nation. We are literally drowning in pornography: It is now a multimillion-dollar business. Ten years ago much of it was imported. But today the U.S. is the biggest exporter of filth in all the world.

With its television shows and VCR movies, our nation has developed an appetite for perversion and sado-masochism. Even daytime soap operas are full of smut, fornication and homosexuality. TV has become the open floodgate of this barrage of filth.

God is doing to America what He did to Israel after she lusted for flesh in the desert. "Ye shall not eat one day, nor two days, nor five days...until it come out at your nostrils, and it be loathsome unto you" (Num. 11:19,20).

The United States of America is now known as "the nation where anything goes!" There are virtually no more restraints. Young 11- and 12-year-old boys are becoming rapists. *Girls are getting pregnant at age 12 — and then having abortions! Our nation plays the harlot while looking down the barrel of the deadly gun of AIDS, and laughs, "Who's afraid of AIDS?" Last week a movie star confessed that 12 of his best friends have died of AIDS. But he doesn't intend to change his ways!*

4 A MASSIVE DEPRESSION FROM WHICH THERE IS NO ESCAPE. *Many don't like to hear about the coming economic collapse. The word "depression" scares Americans. But believe it or not, we are not just facing another recession that will last a short while before the economy bounces back. Rather, we are facing the last great depression!*

It happened to every past society and empire in the throes of judgment. Don't believe it won't happen to us. Because of Israel's unfaithfulness, the Lord said to that nation: "Thou hast multiplied thy merchants above the stars of heaven: the cankerworm spoileth, and fleeth away" (Nah. 3:16).

In this prophecy, the prophet Nahum was warning the city of an insidious enemy that would come to destroy its economy. Nineveh exported glassworks, textiles, carpets, ivory carvings, artwork of all kinds, gems, silver, gold and spices. Its merchants traveled throughout the world. But before long an invading cancer came, and enemies swooped down, spread themselves over the rich spoil and fled with the loot.

Rest assured the day is not far off when Japan, Taiwan, Korea and Germany will take their money from the United States and flee! "All they that look upon thee shall flee from thee, and say, Nineveh is laid waste: who will bemoan her? whence shall I seek comforters for thee?" (3:7). "All that hear the bruit [news] of thee shall clap the hands over thee: for upon whom hath not thy wickedness passed continually?" (3:19).

One day soon, Japan will quit buying our government bonds — as will all other nations. We will not be able to finance our massive debt. It will all tumble and fall. "He [God] hath caused thine enemy to rejoice over thee" (Lam.\2:17).

The real estate market will crash as well. Zephaniah warned Nineveh: "Desolation shall be in the thresholds" (2:14). The thresholds represent dwellings. He prophesied of empty buildings with birds flying in and out of the shattered windows. "The bittern shall lodge in the upper lintels of it" (verse 14). The New American Standard Bible reads, "Birds will sing in the window."

Even now in Dallas, Houston and Denver we see the appalling sight of empty skyscrapers: "A day of the trumpet and alarm against the fenced cities, and against the high towers" (Zeph. 1:16). High buildings — skyscrapers — in New York City, represent the pride, competition and greed of American society. The day is coming when many of these towers will stand empty like giant, decaying tombstones, full of homeless people.

WHEN WILL ALL THIS FALL UPON US? Nahum said of Nineveh, "The Lord hath given a commandment concerning thee...will I cut off...for thou art vile" (1:14). "I believe God already has given the commandment to bring forth all these prophesied judgments," Dave told me. "It all has been set in motion. The word I keep hearing in my spirit is 'acceleration.' The fire has been ignited — and soon it will grow hotter, more intense and eventually will encompass all our society."

What about the people of God?

What are we facing?

"Nicky, again, we are driven to the Word to find out what the Lord declared and performed in the past. Let's search the Scriptures:

"Noah and his family escaped the flood. Were they preserved? Yes!

"Did Daniel and the Hebrew children survive the furnace and lion's den? Yes!

"Did Lot and those who heeded God's warnings perish in Sodom? No!

"Didn't Jesus warn the Jews to flee Jerusalem when invading armies approached? He said, 'When ye shall see Jerusalem compassed with armies ... flee to the mountains ... depart out; and let not them that are in the countries enter' (Luke 21:20,21). Jerusalem was destroyed while the obedient ones escaped — remembering the Lord's warning.

"EVEN TO THE WICKED NINEVEH, for the sake of even one righteous man, God gave this glorious message: 'The Lord is good, a stronghold in the day of trouble; and He knoweth them that trust in Him' (Nahum 1:7). Those who listen and obey have always been saved!

"His stronghold is a fortified house of rock: 'In Thee, O Lord, do I put my trust...be Thou my strong rock, for an house of defense to save me. For Thou art my rock and my fortress' (Psalm 31:1-3).

"And here is how we will be kept safe:

"'Into Thine hand I commit my spirit: Thou hast redeemed me, O Lord God of truth...Thou hast known my soul in adversities; and hast not shut me up into the hand of the enemy: Thou hast set my feet in a large room' (31:5, 7-8).

"Nicky, the time has come for you and me to preach an urgent message: *Prepare now for God's imminent judgments — by setting your heart on the Rock who provides refuge for His own.* Commit the keeping of your body and soul to our gracious and merciful Lord."

Yes, how true.

HOW GOD INTENDS TO SAVE HIS PEOPLE in these troubled times, I do not know — but with Him nothing is impossible. He is our ark of safety, so we need not fear, or run, or hide. Even if we leave this world by way of a hydrogen meltdown, it will be instant deliverance from a world gone mad.

"Call me a doomsayer," Dave told me. "Call me unpatriotic — call me any name you please. But I am already a citizen of another country — the New Jerusalem, which is above. We are supposed to be looking for a city whose builder and maker is God.

"Jesus forewarned us of a day coming — so frightful, men's hearts would fail them for fear, beholding the horrors coming on the earth.

"Then, He said, *'Look up and rejoice, for your redemption draws near.'" (see Luke 21:28).*

Chapter 15

More
Important
Things

"WE DO KNOW HOW many people in our congregation who are stricken with AIDS," Dave told me. "Some of them have already died. Two of them died this past month. We have homeless people, we have three men in the choir who have lost executive jobs. They are people trying to meet their rent. I just had a mother here with her 16-year-old boy who is a drug pusher.

"People have incredible problems and just being their pastor keeps me occupied. I don't have time for the deep doctrinal issues anyway. I don't have time to argue with anyone about theology. I go home with my guts burning in me because of a little 16-year-old girl our people took in off the streets just days ago. She was selling her body doing porno films."

I KNEW WHAT HE MEANT. Just days before, 33-year-old Greg Vaughn, the popular basketball coach at Brooklyn's Prospect Heights High School had been killed in a terrible gang incident that grabbed the headlines.

A friendly 6-foot-6 athlete who loved kids, Greg had left his coaching job at Medgar Evers College to return to our decaying Brooklyn neighborhoods — where he spent a lot of time going around to playgrounds, trying to persuade kids to stay in school at Prospect Heights High and off of drugs.

Basketball was his gimmick.

He was the all-time leading scorer and rebounder at Queens College on the other side of the city — and so, one fateful afternoon, he had agreed to referee a Queens neighborhood league game at Baisley Pond Park, an area ruled by a drug-trafficking street gang called the Supreme Team.

Little did Greg know that the sneering, high-rolling punks of the gang had bet $50,000 among themselves on the outcome of the game.

SO, WHEN GREG MADE A DISPUTED CALL in the last minutes of the contest, disallowing a basket by the team that was losing by a single point, he was jumped.

Queens police say none of the neighborhood kids or players will admit to seeing anything. But the coroner says Greg was punched three times in the head before he fell unconscious to the concrete.

He never got up.

Five days later, he died in a local hospital.

He made the mistake of believing that something wholesome and good like basketball could make a difference. "In the '60s and '70s, young guys coming up had a choice, drugs or basketball," one of Greg's friends, Fred

Patasaw, told the *New York Daily News*. "Now, drugs run the game."

Indeed, a policeman in Harlem told the newspaper that 85 per cent of the summer sports leagues are funded by street drug gangs — which then cash in on the gambling that they generate on the outcome.

We're talking about kids' games here — not the *Giants* or the *Yankees* or *Mets, Nets* or *Knickerbockers*.

Kids.

Whose playground fun has been prostituted into the sleeze of point-spreads and odds favorites by drug-funded bookmakers. And they are just doing the same thing that the adults have legitimized over the years. Put a little money on the game. Had a little "harmless fun."

That fun killed Greg Vaughn.

And his strong voice against drugs and gangs was silenced.

Oh, yes, New York has changed.

"LOOK AT THE THOUSANDS of people sleeping in the streets," Dave told me. "It changes you, I've changed."

Not far from Times Square Church just nights before, police vice officers working undercover had bought crack cocaine from two street pushers during one of the periodic efforts to clean up the streets.

As officers rushed in to arrest the two, another young man stepped from the shadows and offered to sell them another vial of crack. They arrested him, too. It was a successful operation — but police admit that those sorts of arrests have little effect on the drug trade.

The sellers are back on the street before arresting officers have finished their paperwork. And for every drug trafficker sent away to do hard time in overcrowded prisons, three more step out of the shadows to take over his turf.

"The kids know they are going to get busted, and there is a fair chance they may be killed," said one policeman. "But the financial incentives are so strong that they don't seem to care."

In a recent 12-month period, more than 1,850 murders were committed in New York City. Many of them were drug related.

"I don't care if people call me a prophet or anything," says Wilkerson. "That's not going to help me on the streets right outside these doors here. We have 50,000 homeless people here — 50,000.

"The newspaper said we have 70,000 to 80,000 people going absolutely insane on crack. Nicky, God has given me my call. Somebody else will have to do the theological arguing.

"My job is to give these hurting people Jesus Christ and to wage spiritual battle in the devil's backyard.

"That's what I'm doing, Nicky."

His heart-cry touched me. That evening on network news, the mayor of Washington, D.C., was facing new disgrace and drug charges. New statistics showed that the cocaine plague is doubling in intensity — even in small-town America. Federal drug czar William Bennett quoted new statitstics showing that one out of every 40 New York City residents is a frequent user of cocaine.

I wept.

NOW, I ALSO HAVE A BURDEN like never before for this city of my youth. This is still my city. The whole religious world seems to be converging on the newly opened countries of the former Eastern Bloc — and my heart cries out that nobody seems to care about what's happening here.

We have a war in our midst — drugs, gangs, witchcraft and violence like never before.

We must answer the call.

I know I must. The urgency moves me so deeply that my stomach is in knots. My heart is heavy with pain.

Lord, let me answer the call.

Show me the way.

Section IV

The Battle Before Us

Chapter 16

How to Win the War Against Drugs

IN THE DARK STREETS of my great city, there's a 22-year-old prostitute who calls herself Bambi.

Tonight, you will find her and thousands like her on the city's dangerous sidewalks.

She's leaning up against a white-painted, three-story brick tenement that was once an elegant Victorian apartment house.

Now many of its windows are boarded up, its lights darkened.

Few tenants remain.

The owner lives in Tokyo.

Inside, kids are smoking crack.

Although Bambi is noticeably pregnant, she is still a frequent client of this "crack house" between sexual encounters with her customers in parked cars or filthy hotel rooms.

At the back door, she clears her throat and a dark-eyed man lets her in. There, she doesn't count the other addicts crouching in the gutted hallway, inhaling the drug that is her reason for living.

Nor does she brag that most of the $500-750 she earns nightly goes to buying crack.

The dark-eyed man leads her up an unlit stairway and into a second-floor kitchen.

The furniture is broken crates and an overturned, slashed sofa with filthy stuffing spilling out onto the garbage-strewn floor.

Bambi buys a vial of white cocaine powder — a treat, "the real thing," not the crystalline crack that has become so popular.

She dissolves the drug into water in a dirty tablespoon, then tears away the filter from her half-smoked cigarette, dipping it carefully in the concoction.

She says that the filter draws away impurities that could kill her.

Her theory is without basis in fact.

Many die daily.

Filling a hypodermic needle with liquid, she rolls up her sleeve and inserts the needle into her arm where large scabs have formed from repeated injections.

She begins to cry in frustration when she cannot find a healthy vein into which to inject the soothing, exciting elixir that will bring peace and euphoria for about 10 minutes.

Then, she is back outside.

Within a half-hour, she will have hustled up enough money for another fix.

This time all she can afford is crack — rock cocaine.

Agitated, she will be back inside, poking a 7-Up soft-drink can with a bent nail and piling crack rocks around the hole.

Then, she ignites the rocks and draws the smoke through the side of the can.

It's awkward, but she has no cocaine pipe.

It and others like it have been confiscated in her many run-ins with police. They do not release it with her other personal belongings when she is released from jail — *paraphernalia* is finally now illegal.

For years it was not.

But as officials belatedly undertook to battle the drug epidemic, they finally realized that it made very little sense to allow any shopkeeper in the city to sell devices with which to smoke, inhale, scoop up or mix the drugs killing a generation.

BAMBI DOES NOT KNOW JESUS.

She knows cocaine.

It is her only friend.

She will sell herself many times this night to get cocaine. She probably has the AIDS virus, but that's of little concern to her.

Nor is she about to warn her sexual partners.

She needs cocaine and will do whatever is necessary to get it.

A mother not far from here was charged recently with holding down a 6-year-old daughter while three men raped the child.

In return, the mother was given enough crack for a high.

A FEW WEEKS AGO Dave visited the Teen Challenge farm in Pennsylvania, where 200 former junkies and alcoholics live, free from chemical abuse and the perversions of the city.

What a night it was. They all came up on stage and began to sing the chorus *"I'm Free, I'm Free, Jesus Set Me Free."*

As Dave looked at those former addicts, alcoholics and abusers, he told me he saw the joy of Jesus just radiating from them.

"And I thought, there is the real war on drugs. No amount of money can do this," he said.

The following Friday night he spoke in Manchester, New Hampshire, for another drug program, *New Life for Girls.*

They had an all-girl choir there, all converted drug addicts.

Government officials were there from the state of New Hampshire.

So were the the mayor, some legislators, and people from various groups of psychology programs and local colleges and college students.

THE OUTSIDERS WERE SO SKEPTICAL. They sat there with their hands folded.

But Dave began to smile to himself as he watched their attitudes change — as those beautiful girls transformed by the blood of Jesus began to get up and testify, one after another.

One girl said, "I was bound by drugs, had no hope and Jesus set me free. Now I have a job and out of eight applicants, I was accepted because they saw something special in me, they said."

The girls began to tell about being restored to their families.

They began to talk about the desire for drugs being lifted by the power aof the Holy Spirit.

They were beautiful women.

They had been prostitutes, alcoholics and addicts, and now are clean, washed and pure by the blood of Jesus Christ.

There is the war on drugs!

The Bible says, "Oh, that my people had hearkened unto Me ... I would soon have subdued their enemies," (Ps. 81:13,14).

But as Dave sat there and watched those ladies, he knew:

This is how we will win the war on drugs.

No, governments will not win the battle on drugs. They don't have the tools.

Chapter 17

Come to the
War Zone

"WE ARE LIVING IN SOME of the most perilous times in history," Dave recently proclaimed to his congregation. "The President of the United States once again has declared war on drugs, saying that we are striving to save the soul of this society.

"But, our world is diseased in its heart."

TODAY, ENTIRE COUNTRIES in South America and Southeastern Asia are run by drug lords feeding our consumer society's craving for an illicit high. It's just as bad in Holland and England and Germany and Denmark as it is in New York City.

So, how can we hope to win this battle against drugs? First, says Dave, we cannot believe what we see with our human eyes. We cannot see the true war.

"THE DISEASE AFFECTS US ALL. We see children falling on the right and the left. We see young people turning to drugs by the thousands. May God give us a burden, give every Christian a broken heart, not just to weep over the problem, but to study God's Word to see what the solution is from His heart. Our God is the only one with the solution."

That may seem too pat, too easy, too religious an answer for some.

After all, the solutions seem immensely complex. The drug problem has reached crisis proportions in Greenland and ... yes, Los Angeles, Liverpool, Honolulu, Budapest, Detroit, Bern, Bonn, Bogota, Bangkok, Rome, London, Miami, Belfast, Washington, D.C., Amsterdam, Paris and Chicago. It's a growing problem in Tokyo, Tel Aviv, Brasilia, Prague, Buenos Aires and Moscow.

And it has overrun some small countries.

BOLIVIA IS TWICE THE SIZE of Texas, the fifth largest country in South America. Desperately poor, the land-locked Andes Mountains country has suffered 188 political overthrows since Spain granted independence in 1825.

Bolivia is divided into three distinct regions:

• The altiplano, a harsh plateau atop the Andes, where most of the country's native Inca-descended majority live in abject poverty.

• The yungas, fertile valleys that make up the country's agricultural heartland, farmed by *mestizos* or mixed-blood descendants of the Incas and Spaniards.

• The llanos (lowlands), the power base of Bolivia's minority "Europeans," who are mainly of German and Spanish descent.

In the early 1970s, Bolivia suffered a series of devastating economic disasters: the price of its chief export, tin, nosedived. Explorations for oil proved only that the country was completely without such resources. Then, the wealthy landowners of the Santa Cruz region were encouraged by the government to plant heavily in cotton for export.

In 1974, the government-run Banco Agricola invested 52 per cent of its available cash in new cotton fields, most of it in unsecured loans. But just as those cotton fields matured, world cotton prices plummeted. As a result, most of Banco Agricola's clients went into default.

THEY SAVED THEMSELVES and perhaps their country by quickly replanting their fields with coca — the sturdy weed from which cocaine is produced. This ingenious crop substitution campaign was conducted by the Santa Cruz chapter of the *Asociación de Productores de Algodón,* the local cotton producers' association. It was done on such a colossal scale that it is difficult to believe that it happened without at least the passive nonintervention of the Bolivian government.

After all, the entire country was on the verge of bankruptcy.

The result was that Bolivia's coca crop boomed from 11,000 tons in 1973 to 35,000 tons in 1978. Did the government know? In order to make export possible, coca farmers have to process their leaves, extracting the potent alkaloids from the leaves with vast quantities of sulfuric acid, alcohol and acetone — all of which had to be imported.

Roads, railways and 3,000 airstrips were necessary to transport the chemicals in and the coca paste out to Colombia where it was turned to cocaine and sent on to the United States.

All of this was done as Bolivia's government loudly proclaimed its cooperation with international efforts to halt the flood of death.

For most Bolivians, the consequences of the coca revolution were disastrous as normal agriculture went into a decline, Only a few reaped the benefits: $400 worth of coca leaves became $2,000 worth of coca paste, then $15,000 worth of cocaine in Colombia — and worth $65,000 once it was smuggled across the U.S. border, then worth $300,000 or more on the street.

Various Bolivian governments — they rarely last more than eight months — have cooperated with international officials and U.S. drug agents to stem the tide of coca paste. Massive campaigns such as Operation Blow Torch in 1986 spend millions, eradicate thousands of acres of illicit crops, destroy hundreds of clandestine labs and confiscate entire small air forces of cargo planes. But the coca industry always bounces back.

THE REALITIES OF GREED, free market economics and human nature rule: If a farmer can be dirt-poor raising cotton or fabulously wealthy raising coca leaves, only the man of highest moral fiber will refuse to rationalize the risks and ethics of meeting the demand for cocaine — particularly as the price goes up.

And this is only the situation in Bolivia. It is far, far worse in Burma, Cambodia, Thailand, Peru, Colombia and Mexico.

Dave says he doesn't want to criticize any effort various governments are trying to put forth about the drug problem.

"For three decades, government leaders have talked about doing something effective, but didn't do it," said Dave. "Now the United States wants to spend $8 billion to declare war on drug lords and pushers and abusers of drugs. That sounds like a lot of money, doesn't it?

"BUT LOOK AT THE $200 BILLION spent that same week to bail out the savings and loan industry. So, $8 billion is not even five per cent of what the government of the United States is going to do for its bankers."

Indeed, who is more important: our youth or our bankers?

"NOW I WANT TO TELL YOU SOMETHING, the war on drugs by any government is doomed. It is absolutely doomed to disaster. What you're going to see will be a cosmetic war. You are going to see a lot of hype, a lot of public relations. You will hear of a few drug lords being extradicted from Bolivia and Colombia and Panama and Thailand. They will be put on trial. They will be given showcase trials. They may even get some years in prison. But it won't even make a dent in the drugs flowing in.

"You are going to see pictures on television and newspapers of Brazilian or Laotian or Burmese or Peruvian or Bolivian troops going in, burning out some of the plantations of the drug lords. You will see pictures of great big heaps of heroin and cocaine being confiscated. It will look like there is some progress being made.

"But, the war on drugs cannot be won by governments, because it is not a physical war.

"It is a spiritual war.

"It is a sin problem."

Chapter 18

Needed:
A Change
of Heart

"IT WAS IMPOSSIBLE to get high anymore or to stop," says the 31-year-old former New York City addict.

To look at him, you would scoff at the notion that the robust, well-dressed professional ever had a drug problem.

After all, Jim is a medical doctor, a graduate of a leading medical school and a former New York City resident in anesthesiology — a specialty that he says he chose in medical school specifically because it would give him access to drugs.

But he is not alone. According to David Smith, an authority on drug abuse and the founder of the Haight-Ashbury Free Medical Clinic in San Francisco, "the toll among anesthesiologists is so high that addiction is now considered an occupational hazard."

In two recent studies of addiction among 173 anesthesiologists, 37 had died as the result of drug addiction.

Abuse is so common that users have their own street-type lingo — such as a "party pack," enough morphine to anesthesize a patient for minor surgery ... which also happens to be enough for three friends on the golf course to get really plastered.

"In the last stages of my addiction, I needed eight or 10 shots a day," remembers Jim.

HE STARTED USING MORPHINE as a medical student when a patient at the teaching hospital had an incredibly ecstatic reation to morphine administered before a painful procedure. He pocketed the leftover drug and injected it into his arm later. "From that point on," he remembers, "I never threw narcotics away."

Drugs became a big part of his life — helping him stay alert and energetic through graduation, then enabling him to withstand the rigors of hospital residency, where young doctors are often expected to put in 24- and 36-hour shifts.

"The addicted doctor doesn't just suddenly show up loaded one day at work," says Will Spiegelman, an anesthesiologist at Stanford University Hospital and an addiction specialist. "It's a progressive disease. By the time he starts functioning poorly at the hospital — at least two years and often more after he's become addicted — he's practically dead."

FOR JIM, FEEDING HIS ENORMOUS habit — and quelling his desperate fears that his supply of morphine would be interrupted — produced paranoia of the worst kind. Terrified that colleagues might detect something was wrong with him, Jim became exhausted, isolated and depressed. He lost touch with his family and withdrew from friends as his self-esteem vanished.

He had started with only two or three milligrams of morphine to get high. But now, all he wanted to do was function like a normal human being. His all-consuming goal was to walk the thin edge between the agonies of withdrawal and the death of overdose — for getting high was no longer that important.

Staying alive was.

Incredibly, Jim was not caught by friends, family, police or fellow doctors. During an audit of the hospital's drug supplies, a computer brought Jim's name to the top of the list of doctors procuring drugs. Hospital officials were taken aback by Jim's enormous volume of written prescriptions — all supposedly for patients.

JIM WAS CALLED IN FOR QUESTIONING and only then did hospital officials spot telltale signs that he was using the drugs himself. Forced to submit to a urine test, he deftly substituted a drug-free patient's sample for his own.

Declared clean, he promised to quit overprescribing narcotics for his patients. And he turned to buying drugs on the street. He volunteered for high-paying overtime in the emergency room so he could afford the street drugs — increasing his intake and his physical exhaustion so that he was having to inject himself more and more often in the hospital restroom stalls, where he ran the serious threat of being caught.

Eventually, however, he ran out of money and returned to writing phony prescriptions. This time, the hospital computer was watching him. Alarms went off.

He was forced into a detoxification program — although he continued to deny any addiction.

Today Jim is drug-free.

After scoffing at the idea that he was in the same category as the addicted teens and adult alcoholics in encounter sessions at the detoxification program, he finally saw the truth. He admitted to himself that he was a junkie.

And then the healing began.

In a chapel service, he began to listen to what the chaplain was saying. At the altar that evening, he asked God to help him fight a battle that he could not win alone.

And he was given the strength to stand alone.

And that is how the war on drugs will be won.

When we win men's hearts.

"WE ARE GOING TO TRY TO INDUCE the Colombians and Bolivians to grow oranges instead of coca leaves, from which comes the cocaine. But it is not going to stop anything," Dave Wilkerson told me.

"And I'll tell you what, Nicky, even if they were able to stop every ton of heroin, every drop of crack, if they stopped all of these drugs that are pouring in from all of our borders — if they could stop them overnight, it wouldn't help!

"THE FORCES OF WICKEDNESS would come up with designer drugs, synthetic designer drugs, like this new 'ice' that is on the streets right now. It can be made in a laboratory and $1 billion worth can be put in one box. It's 2,000 times more powerful than crack."

If you think crack has taken the nation by storm, just wait for designer drugs to spread — particularly if the Coast Guard, U.S. Customs, the Drug Enforcement Agency and the armed forces somehow succeed to block the flow of marijuana, cocaine and opiates into the United States.

A favorite already on the streets of New York is fentanyl — with a wallop 100 times as strong as morphine and 50 times as potent as heroin. It's a synthetic drug, altered by underground chemists just slightly to get by federal drug statutes.

The law carefully defines the chemistry of what is illegal. So, designer drugs are custom-built to get the user high, but skirt the law. When they first hit the street, they are completely legal.

It took officials long months to decide whether to ban the controversial designer drug "ecstacy" since it was not an illegal compound, did not seem to be addictive and apparently heightened a number of positive traits, such as affection and introspection. Some designer drugs are incredible. Sufentanyl and lofentanyl are said to be as much as 6,000 times as strong as morphine. But there are terrible risks. Since the drugs are altered forms of known narcotics, they have unknown new characteristics — sometimes have terrible side effects. For example, at least 107 people died from a batch of meperidine that was botched by the basement chemist and contained the compound MPTP — which contained a deadly neurotoxin. About 400 known survivors now have a syndrome like Parkinson's Disease.

According to *Discovery* magazine writer Winifred Gallagher, "The flood of designer drugs portends that in the not-so-distant future, there may no longer be any demand for botanical narcotics, nor any need for the elaborate criminal networks that supply them."

"If you're in the Mafia," says G. Douglass Talbott, head of the Impaired Physicians Program in Atlanta, "you may as well get out of the business."

And that makes the government's war on drugs seem a little silly.

ALL OF THE POWER of the United States government, says Dave, all the technology of the British military and all the determination of the Australian or Canadian or German police cannot take away the desire for drugs. "How can a program be successful when they can't change the heart of man?" Dave asks.

"Why do we have this dreadful, frightful plague of drugs and alcohol, especially among our young people? Thousands of babies being born addicted to their drug-addicted mothers — many premature, many with brain damage — and frail and sickly?"

Why is it happening with such intensity?

WHERE DID IT COME FROM? Even 9- and 10-year-old kids in New York City are pushing drugs. Police picked up an 8-year-old boy in fact, up in Harlem with a little paper sack with 400 vials of crack he was selling. Eight years old!

"Our kids laugh at 'Just Say No,'" says Dave. "Right in my face, young teens scoff and tell me, 'Just say no to all my gold chains and this $5,000 wristwatch? Say no to these designer clothes and go back to nothing? To food stamps and Salvation Army used clothes?'"

Dave shakes his head and sighs.

THESE ARE KIDS that were in poverty a few months ago. The problem is that death doesn't even scare them anymore. Try going up to any of these teen-agers now that are using the drugs they sell, and you tell them they are going to die very soon probably with a bullet in their head in the gutter.

"They will say, 'So what! I was dead anyhow. My dad's an alcoholic, my mom's on drugs and doesn't care, I lived with my grandma and didn't have any money, dropped out of school. And if I'm going to die with a bullet in my head, I'm going out in style. I'll have some money in my pocket, I'll be driving a nice car and if I go to Hell, I'm going to Hell in a Porsche.'"

WHAT IS HAPPENING — how is it that the world's richest city has become a prostitute to drugs? "Teen-agers on New York's streets who were once penniless, tool around in fancy sports cars," says Dave. "They have Jeeps, Corvette convertibles equipped with $3,000 stereos. They wear gold chains and they pull out big wads of $100 bills." And they carry guns — because their life expectancy is so short. Hiding in every shadow, somebody is waiting to kill them, steal their pretties, and take over their turf.

What's happened?

"I had one boy say, 'I make $2,000 a day. Just say no? Right, man!'"

Worse still are the parents turning to selling coke and crack to pay off their mortgages and keep up with their neighbors.

"I had a mother stop me two weeks ago. Her young teen saw one of his best friends blown away by somebody to whom he owed money for the drugs he was selling.

"Now, that boy is selling drugs!"

Even after seeing his best friend die?

"I CAN'T REALLY GIVE IT UP," the boy told Dave. "I'll never use any of these drugs, but selling them is my ticket out of here! I've never had so much money!"

"I couldn't touch him," says Dave sadly. He couldn't hear the wise warning that he will probably never see his 17th birthday.

"And did you read yesterday in the *New York Daily News,* about the mother in Queens who told police she had financial pressure and saw all of her neighbors driving these nice cars and wondered where they were coming from. And they said, 'Easy,' and introduced her to one of the pushers. She became a contact.

"Then, she started using her product and got hooked. She owed her supplier a lot of money and couldn't pay it. So, she gave her 13-year-old daughter to the pusher to take to his rowdy crowd of men to rape and molest. They abused her for a week."

There is a terrible pain in Dave's eyes as he tells the story.

"What is behind this curse on this society?"

FIRST OF ALL, OUR LEADERS and officials have rejected the Lord as the only true source of help, he says. "You know, we have legislators, we have Supreme Court judges, we have humanistic people in high places who laugh at the idea of a God who will gladly fight this battle for us — if we will only humble ourselves and ask Him. They do not even consider God as an intelligent option anymore!

"They are so committed to human lies that they can win in their own strength! They are determined to find their own solutions! They would rather see this civilization die than turn to God. They would rather their country go down the tubes than be 'weak' and turn to 'religion' as an answer. They cannot admit they need God as their source of help. They'd rather lose the war."

And that's exactly what will happen.

"I READ IN THE PAPER," Dave continued, "how the President of the United States called the Prime Minister of England, he called the leaders of France, Holland and Colombia. He called most of South America and he called the leaders of Peru and he asked them to please help America save its soul.

"We'll turn to world leaders — but not to God. The President has made a call to the Pope begging for help. Look what we are doing: We are reaching to world leaders, we are reaching to our experts, we are reaching to the Pope, but we close our eyes to the truth. If the solution is God, then we don't want it.

"We have pushed Him out of our schools. We have pushed Him out of our courts. We have designed Him out of our laws."

AND HE'S BEEN PUSHED out of many of our churches. We have said God is not even an option — we're too sophisticated and scientific to stoop to asking the Creator of the universe for help! Then we wonder why we are being left alone in the darkness, left to a vengeful Lucifer delighted at the chance to destroy us.

"You see, when we denied God and rejected Him in our society we left ourselves morally and spiritually bankrupt. We have created a vacuum in which the devil has moved with all of his henchmen.

"In all of history, any nation that relied on God to fight its battles and turned to Him with all of its heart was absolutely invincible. Look at what happened when a prayerful America joined World War II! The evil tide of Nazism was turned back!

"NO ENEMY CAN COME into the borders of a nation protected by God. No enemy can oppose His protection.

"When a nation is right with God, the Bible says, no one can stand before them. Your enemies that rise up against you shall be smitten before your face. They shall come out against you one way, they'll flee before you seven ways. That was God's message at one time. *You just walk in humility before Me, you seek My face, you turn in righteousness to Me. You humble yourself before Me and trust in Me and let Me be your help! Look to Me for your salvation, look to Me to fight your battles.* And God said that your enemies will flee seven ways before you.

"BUT LET ME SHOW YOU what happens when a nation sins and rejects God just as ancient Israel did. They turned away from the God who won their battles and decided to take things into their own hands. Here is the result: *The Lord shall cause thee to be smitten before thine enemies. Thou shalt go out one way against Him and you will flee seven ways before your enemies. Your carcass shall be meat to the fowls of the air.*

"That is exactly where we are right now."

Chapter 19

Needed:
Prayer
Warriors

DAVE SPEAKS THE WORDS OF JESUS. They sound hard in this lazy, self-centered society. Yet, they are filled with such wise warnings.

Dave does not announce his latest whim, wrapping it in religious words and defensively proclaiming "Thus saith the Lord." No, his Jeremiads do not come easily; this is not a man of idle words. I have watched Dave moan and groan before the Lord for hours — particularly if the Holy Spirit is birthing in him a hard message for the people God loves.

I remember the first time that I ever watched him humbling himself before the Lord. I'd just become a Christian and Dave knew he had to get me out of Brooklyn — for the temptations and dangers were too great. He took me home with him, then to upstate New York — where I immediately got into trouble with the law.

SURE, I'D BEEN SAVED IN A DRAMATIC WAY. But I was still Nicky Cruz, Puerto Rican street kid, emotional orphan, an adolescent with zero self-esteem, whose self-worth had been found in the violent thrills of flowing blood and the drunken, lusty orgies of gang life. In little Elmira, NY, I immediately attracted the attentive eye of the local police. Although I had done nothing but swagger around the city park in my gang jacket, the small-town cops gave Dave 24 hours to get me out of town.

That evening, Dave knelt in the darkness of his room, talking aloud to nobody that I could see. He began moaning and groaning, weeping and as far as I could tell, he was wandering off into the *Twilight Zone.*

"Hey, man," I whispered shaking his shoulder. "What's wrong with you?"

He looked up at me in surprise. "I'm praying," he said simply.

For the next several hours, I watched him pray as only Dave Wilkerson prays. He prostrated himself before the Almighty and completely opened his heart and soul to the great Lord who is his mighty Friend.

I WAS SO TOUCHED — for Dave's pain was on my behalf. He told God about it in human words and then in moanings and groanings straight out of Romans 8:26, John 11:38 and 2 Corinthians 5:2. All three passages — as well as numerous psalms — tell of times when our great hurts and burdens simply cannot be expressed in man's inadequate languages.

Then, Dave stood, refreshed and at peace. "Don't worry," he told me, "God has everything under control." Sure enough, as the last minutes ticked away for me to get out of Elmira, an elderly couple showed up at the house. They said simply that the Lord had told them to come get me and take me into their home in another town. I was astounded.

But I saw how Dave handles confrontation and crisis. He lets God fight his wars. When the Lord orders him into battle, he is obedient. But Dave knows who is doing the real fighting.

Perhaps someday God will cause me to be the prayer warrior that Dave Wilkerson is. I must admit that I am envious of anyone who has such a hotline to the throne room of Heaven. Oh, yes, God has given me a different anointing in which I am content.

But I have never been or even known a prayer warrior like Dave.

I REMEMBER ONCE WHEN DAVE WAS holding a crusade in Chicago. I was just a young Christian. Former drug addict Sonny Arguinzoni and I were traveling with Dave, who was not getting much sleep because Sonny snores like a buzz saw.

One night in particular, it was awful. Sonny sounded like a small plane coming in for a landing. He shook the room. I was sure he was bringing the whole city of Chicago down around us. Somehow I finally got to sleep.

But around 6 a.m., I awoke with a start.

Sonny still sounded like an earthquake in progress but Dave was gone.

I jumped up.

Quietly I began searching the nursing home where we were staying. Panicking, I searched every room, even the basement and the closets. Suddenly it hit me: *Oh, no! Jesus has returned! Dave has been taken and I've been left behind!*

I saw his bed was made, his pajamas folded, his slippers in place. Everything was immaculate. My heart began to beat fast. Tearing up to our room, I woke Sonny. As calmly as possible, I told him urgently: "Sonny, Jesus has come. I don't know what you and I have done that is so terrible, but we've been left. Dave's with Jesus."

Stricken, Sonny jumped out of bed and we both fell to our knees. Crying, convinced that we had missed the Second Coming of Jesus, we began pleading with the Lord to give us another chance. Sonny began confessing his sins. Beside him, I was about to detail a number of terrible sins that I had never told anybody when —to my immense relief— Dave strolled in.

As he looked at us, then listened to what we thought had happened, he got tickled. It is one of the few times I've ever seen him overcome with hilarity. We giggled and guffawed as he chortled and chuckled and pounded us on the back until we were all laughing and crying together at the same time.

Dave had just slipped out for a few private, intimate hours with the Lord.

I was greatly relieved.

And once again, I was impressed that I could not slack off in my intimacy with our Lord. His is the only strength that counts. His is the only wisdom that is real. Without Him, I was fighting in the dark against enemies that we cannot see.

With Him, our human foolishness is transformed. In our weakness, we are — or can be—mighty. And in humility, we can see the absolute sovereignty of a great God who loves us greatly.

But if we reject Him — the consequences are terrible.

Such as we see on the streets of New York City today.

"WE ARE UNDER THE ROD of God's chastening for our rejection of the Lord," Dave says. "God permits wicked enemies to serve as His rod of correction and chastisement. I'm telling you now that our nation is under the rod of

God. He says, 'I'll cause you to pass under the rod.' He said, 'As I pleaded with your fathers, so I will plead with you, and I'll cause you to pass under the rod.'

"Violence has risen up like a rod of wickedness. The Scriptures say that if we forsake His law and if we break His statutes and we keep not His commandments, *then will I visit your transgressions with the rod and with iniquity and your iniquity with strifes.*

"Do you remember when God judged Israel by sending the Assyrian Army to be His rod, to do His correcting of Israel? The Assyrians were the rod of His anger, the staff in the hand of His indignation.

"GOD SAID, 'I'M ANGRY AT YOU and I'm going to let these Assyrians come in and I'm going to let them invade your land. I'm going to let them move in among you and I'm going to use them as a rod.'

"And that's exactly what is happening to us with the drug lords, drug pushers, and the pimps and the prostitutes here. They have become the rod of God to chastise our wicked society."

Chapter 20

A Matter of Reputation

DAVE TOLD OF A YOUNG LADY, Mary, who stopped him after a recent service. She was once part of the drug world, but was smiling from ear to ear. He had announced that he was going to preach from Psalm 37, she opened her Bible and pointed to two of her favorite verses in that psalm and, according to Dave, said:

"'Brother Wilkerson, when I was on drugs and got saved, I said, 'O, Lord, how do I know I won't fall? How do I know I won't go back? Brother Wilkerson, I'm so glad you're preaching from Psalm 37 because, look, I've got it marked up — all these promises!'

"'**IT WAS GOD TELLING ME,** proving to me that even if I fell, He would not forsake me. I don't have to be afraid of a fall. I don't plan it, but if the devil should trip me up, I'm not going to stay down! The Lord is going to pick me up.'

"The point is," said Dave, "while God declares war on all the workers of iniquity, and He fights against them, He's going to be simultaneously fighting for you and me.

"READ AGAIN VERSES 23 AND 24, *'The steps of a good man are ordered by the Lord: and he delighteth in his way. Though he fall, he shall not be utterly cast down: for the Lord upholdeth him with his hand.'*

"While God has declared war on this iniquitous system, something is happening in Heaven for you and me right now. The devil stands against you and me — accusing you before God.

"And Satan stands there especially when you fail God. When you have stumbled or fallen, Satan stands before the throne of God as an accuser and says, 'All right, he has sinned. The wages of sin is death. That's Your own law. Justice stands before God and justice has a voice.' Justice says, it's true, they have all sinned and fallen short of the glory of God and justice declares there has to be a penalty for sin.

"So, here's the devil accusing you, saying you'll not make it, that he has every right to claim your soul now, that your soul is his.

"AND JUSTICE STANDS THERE and agrees with him. But, my Bible says that Jesus is before the Father as an intercessor. He's not on His knees. He stands on authority to the sprinkling of His own blood on the mercy seat. The devil stands and accuses you, and justice says, 'Yes, the penalty has to be paid.' But Jesus steps in before the Father. He says, 'Yes, there has been a failure. Yes, the law says the penalty has to be paid, but here, I present My blood, I've paid the penalty.'

"All God wants out of the intercession is that we realize that we are accepted into the beloved — not for our own merits or any good enough, but what Jesus has done.

"Jesus stands before the Father and He says, 'This sinner is in My hands. He has has been sprinkled by the blood of the Lamb.' And the Father says, 'Now, Holy Spirit, this is My son, this is My daughter and he is going through a struggle, but I have never loved him more than I love him now. Now You go and comfort and strengthen and guide and bring them through.'

"Hallelujah! Glory to God."

HARD WORDS. WISE WARNINGS that are too easily ignored. Particularly when this man comes under such harsh judgment by those irked by his hard words.

"I listened to a tape I made 25 years ago," he told me. "I wept and cried as I listened to it. It's entitled: *The Making of a Man of God.* It was an awesome experience to listen to myself 25 years ago."

On the tape, he talks about Jesus' pain in the Garden of Gethsemane — a night of confusion and isolation. Jesus went through all of that in the garden. The message was recorded before the rise of today's false message that suffering is the result of sin.

"God did get my attention," Dave told me. "'If I hadn't suffered, I wouldn't have sought the Lord!' King David said.

"I don't think I would be sitting here today, my heart on fire for the Lord had it not been for the suffering we have been through. I really don't know a man of God who has really learned to know Him except through the fellowship of His suffering. It has produced such a dependence on Him. I am more dependent on the Lord now than I have ever been."

AND I LOOK AT WHAT GOD HAS DONE through this man. Look at his fabulous kids — such godly children. Not one of them has turned away from the Lord despite the suffering. So many of my friends in the ministry desperately long to make such a claim. You and I both know good men with seemingly successful ministries — yet, in the back of the auditorium, there is a sneering 15-year-old daughter with her illegitimate baby ... or an angry 32-year-old son who quietly stays away from his dad's crusades since the ministry keeps him on payroll to keep his mouth shut.

This does not mean our children will never become rebellious. Sometimes they rebel just because we and they are always in the public eye. We cannot stop this, but the power of the Holy Spirit can.

I could tell you stories:

• Of the leader of a large ministry whose high school-age son today is a walking time bomb — already accused privately of molesting children in church restrooms. Pray for that boy. This respected author's entire ministry is in danger of tumbling down should he continue to ignore his son's torment.

• Of the major evangelist whose atheist son taught cynicism and doubt along with English at a public high school in his father's hometown — and who died of a drug overdose one night after a party with under-age students.

• Of the young son of a famous family Gospel singing group who at age 13 was taking LSD before each Christian concert and having hallucinations as he played the bass guitar — while everybody thought he was caught up in the Spirit.

But look at Dave's kids. He is no Eli — the Old Testament prophet whose sons were an abomination before the Lord. No, Dave is among those today who can stand with

Billy Graham and proclaim that their children are saved
and following the Lord. All four of Dave's sons and daughters are in ministry. *What a heritage!*

And so, listen with me to these words of my spiritual
dad, hard words — wise warnings:

"LET ME SHOW YOU what the Holy Spirit has revealed
to me and I want you to follow closely," he proclaimed
from his pulpit just a few weeks ago. "All day yesterday the
Holy Spirit was driving this to my heart. The Scripture
says, 'The wicked plot against the innocent.' Look at
Psalm 37:12, *'The wicked plotteth against the just, and
gnasheth upon him with his teeth.'*

"Our forefathers sent out hundreds and thousands of
missionaries. America has always been a missionary nation. So has England. You can go to the hottest jungle of
Africa and you'll find our missionaries. You can go to
Alaska. You can see their works in Inner and Outer Mon-
golia, Ethiopia, Fiji, Haiti, Mauritius, New Guinea, and
even Communist China.

"All over the known world you will find missionaries
our society has sent out. The missionary blood of martyrs
is spread around the world. The devil tried to close the
doors through communism but he couldn't do it. Right
now the doors of communism are swinging wide open.

"God is moving int China.

"God will have a way to get us in.

"THE PRESIDENT IS RIGHT, this is a battle for our
soul. The devil wants the souls of all our young people, all
our potential missionaries, all potential wealth of this
civilization.

"He's also out to destroy the missionary vision that
God gave this people. To absolutely destroy it so that our
kids are not giving themselves anymore to be volunteers

to go to some foreign field, because they will be stoned out of their minds and become spiritual zombies.

"It's an absolute design of the devil that the wicked *plotteth against the righteous, and gnashes against him with his teeth.*

"The devil is gnashing against our people right now because we have brought the peace of Jesus Christ to so many parts of the world. He is trying to totally destroy us.

"*For the rod of the wicked shall not rest upon the lot of the righteous; lest the righteous put forth their hands unto iniquity.*"

"GOD IS NOT MAD AT YOU AND ME," proclaims Dave. "The only ones God is mad at are the devil and his henchmen; He's not mad at you. He's not mad at me. If only you could see the love that He has for you if you're going through a terrible struggle.

"The devil may be trying to strip you and rob you of your confidence in the Lord. Some of you are going through hell in your home. Some of you the devil has whispered in your heart that you're going to fall so badly that you will never make it. Well, just tell the devil that Jesus is praying for you.

"Tell him, *'Jesus is praying for me.'*

"Isn't it wonderful to know that you're not standing up against evil by yourself? Your Heavenly Father sent the Holy Spirit to you.

"Will you receive the Holy Spirit and let Him remind you of the faithfulness of Jesus? Let the Holy Spirit come in right now and speak to your heart, and give you comfort. He will give you the strength to say, "Jesus, You're going to keep me from falling and present me faultless before the throne of God with exceeding great joy.

"Hallelujah!

"DON'T MAKE EXCUSES for your sin. Lay it down. Pray this right out loud from your heart, 'Jesus, I'm ready to surrender. I give up all my self efforts and I trust the Holy Ghost. Touch me, Jesus, and let me see You praying for me, standing with me, helping me, forgiving me, cleansing me and putting Your joy in me. The devil doesn't have me and he can't get me, because I want a wall of fire around me. And I claim that wall right now.'

"Now thank Him for it, right now. 'Thank you, Jesus. Lord I thank You for that wall of fire protecting me.' Glory to Jesus. Glory be to God. Hallelujah!

"Jesus will break all power of the enemy in your life. Ask Him and He will destroy the works of the devil in your heart. Ask him to destroy the works of the devil now and to break through in a mighty way with encouragement, with faith and hope and trust and confidence in the One True God.

"How many believe the Lord is going to take you all the way through all this mess down here today?

"WELL, THE ONLY POWER the devil has over you is his lies — particularly the lies that you are not going to make it. Jesus sees you standing here right now with your heart open. Do you think He's going to turn you down?

"No, if your heart is open and you have a repentant heart, I want you now to take a step in faith and believe the Holy Spirit to come right now and remind you that when your battle gets hot, that when you go back out onto the street where all the demon powers are, the Lord is going to let you walk right through it untouched because He's going to fight your battle.

"He will fight the battle for you. If you walk in harmony with Jesus and come under His yoke, surrendering to His love, to His will, you have nothing to fear.

"ASK THE LORD to take out all your fear, too — to remove all fear in Jesus' Name.

"It doesn't take God all night to do that, my friend.

"When you're ready, He is."

AS I LISTEN, I AM CONVICTED in my heart. Once, I, too judged Dave Wilkerson harshly.

I have never admitted this publicly before.

Our names were often mentioned together in the same breath. When I was introduced, people always called me the punk kid that David Wilkerson brought to the Lord or something like that. The gang leader that Dave Wilkerson rescued in *The Cross and the Switchblade.*

I wanted Dave to speak up and say *"Wait, look what Nicky's become!*

"He's no gang warlord now!

"He's a man of God!

"He's an evangelist!"

As bad as this may seem, I wanted Dave to brag on me.

In my human weakness, I wanted people to know that Dave was proud of me.

I realize that he was.

Oh, *how* proud he was of me.

But he just didn't show it.

I wasn't sure of it, then.

LET ME TELL YOU HOW ELSE I judged Dave even though Dave had been so kind to me as a newborn Christian. I got angry as a young preacher when I thought that he was not very good at discipling young Timothies. I had to go off to Bible college and find my own mentors and shepherds. It seemed to me Dave just didn't take people under his wing and nurture them very often.

Sometimes his word for you is so harsh that you hurt — stunned by his rebuke. It seems that he doesn't care about you — that he hates your sin so intensely.

But that's not the way he is.

I know him.

Dave corrects and rebukes because he loves.

He just may intimidate you.

He can be a scary guy. But I know he's a pussy cat deep inside — a compassionate, caring man with a shepherd's heart. I pray that others will begin to see his gentle side, his caring side — David Wilkerson, the compassionate pastor.

"HOW WILL THE DRUG WAR BE WON?" Dave asks. "God is going to take matters into His own hands. The government's war is pitiful and already lost. But God's war is going to be something awesome, absolutely awesome.

"If we truly repent and return to the faith of our fathers, here's what we can claim from God. Deuteronomy 3:22, *'Ye shall not fear them: for the Lord your God he shall fight for you.'*

What a hard message!

Dave says that if you and I will get where we should be with God, overnight our Mighty Creator will solve the drug crisis. Overnight, the Lord destroyed the Assyrian Army — by sending just one angel.

"TO EVERY DRUG LORD IN COLOMBIA, Laos and Bolivia, wherever they may be, and even here in New York City, to every drug pusher. God says, *'I know where you live.*

"I know your coming in and your going out and I know your rage against Me. Your rage and your tumult has come up into My ears, therefore, I am going to put a hook in your nose and I'll put a bridle on your lips and

I'm going to turn you back by the way which you came. For I am going to defend and save My people for My own sake and for the sake of My servant, David.

"Do you know what God was saying? He was saying to David's enemies, 'I know all your secret plans. I know when you come in or go out.'

"**DO YOU KNOW WHAT** God did in the middle of the night? Israel was completely helpless against the vast Assyrian army. There was no hope.

"But Israel was smart enough to turn to its one source of strength — the Almighty. The one true God. Our Creator and Lord of all that is.

"When God saw their obedience, He sent one angel out and in one night slew 185,000 soldiers.

"Israel came out the next day and there were dead bodies everywhere."

The promises remain.

GOD STANDS READY to deliver His people today, says Dave.

"Do you know if our evil society were to seek God with all of its heart and there was true repentance in the land, God would move in a mighty way.?

"Look what He did in history. Sometimes He confuses the enemy. He makes them fight among themselves. Other times, they die of mysterious plagues. They disappear.

"I'll tell you what, in just 30 days we would look around and the drug problem would be gone. It would be gone!

"**GOD WOULD CLEANSE THE LAND** of all iniquity. He is not going to let drug pushers, pimps and prostitutes and the wicked reign as if He were asleep.

"He's not going to let drug lords sit down in Colombia in their multimillion-dollar mansions. One man down in Colombia has 1,000 prize horses on his ranch. One thousand. There is a general in Burma who has 18,000 personal soldiers pushing drugs. And they laugh at God. They laugh at us. But God is going to say one of these days, 'That's enough.'

"And He's not going to do it because of compassion for a society or a nation or a whole civilization that has turned its back on Him. He's not going to do it because we are worthy.

"He's going to do it for His own Name and the glory of His own Name.

"LET ME READ EZEKIEL 36:21–23 TO YOU, '*But I had pity for mine holy name, which the house of Israel had profaned among the heathen, whither they went....Thus sayeth the Lord God; I do not this for your sakes.*'

"He said, 'I'm not going to do this for you, O Israel, but for My own reputation, which you have defiled. I will not allow the lies about Me to go unanswered. It has been proclaimed throughout history, Israel, that I am your protector. Now, even though you don't deserve it, I will protect you so that the heathen can see that I, indeed, am the Almighty God.

"*I will sanctify my great name...and the heathen shall know that I am the Lord God.*"

Section V

The Battle
Rages On

Chapter 21

The Lord
Will Uphold
the Righteous

READING THE NEWSPAPER in New York City these days, it seems that all you see are pictures of young Brooklyn and Manhattan and Bronx drug pushers lying dead next to their beautiful cars in pools of blood — with a bullet in the back, a bullet in the head.

Over breakfast, Dave held up *The New York Times* for me to see. Floating down some South American river in Peru were 30 headless bodies, all victims in a drug war up in the mountains — a war for turf, however, drug lord versus drug lord.

In the pulpit that evening, Dave was still burdened by what he had read.

"HERE IN THE UNITED STATES now we're seeing terrible things," he proclaimed. "Nicky Cruz, sitting here tonight, was a gang member for years. Years ago, he was a gang leader. He knows this city, better than I do.

"But this time after he flew in from his home in Colorado Springs, he told me, 'Brother Wilkerson, last night I tried to reach you from my hotel. I don't know what's happened to this city, but it's as if there is a terrible darkness, an evil oppression here.'

"He said he struggled with demonic attacks all night. Others I heard today who just came into this city said, 'Brother Wilkerson, what's happened? I feel like running.'

"There's something that happened this year. Satan has come and set up his headquarters right here in this city.

"THERE ARE DEMON SPIRITS LOOSE in this city everywhere we go. But I want you to know something God showed me out of the 37th Psalm.

"God, one of these days, I don't know when it's going to happen, probably overnight, will say, 'That's enough.'

"He's going to declare: 'I'm going to take this war into My own hands.' Look at Psalm 37 verse 9, *'For evildoers shall be cut off: but those that wait upon the Lord, they shall inherit the earth.'*

"The drug traffickers are not going to push us off our inheritance, no way. Read verse 10, *'For yet a little while, and the wicked shall not be: yea, thou shalt diligently consider his place, and it shall not be.'*

"YOU WILL LOOK AROUND and say, 'Where are they? What happened to them? They're gone!' That is in your Bible, too.

"Look at verse 17, *'For the arms of the wicked shall be broken.'* Now if you want to take that literally, that means switchblades and Uzis and assault rifles and machine guns. It means all of their radar equipment and all their fancy equipment to sell and distribute drugs.

"Now, go back to verse 15, *'Their sword shall enter into their own heart, and their bows shall be broken.'*

"WHAT A PROMISE! Now, look at verse 20, *'But the wicked shall perish, and the enemies of the Lord shall be as the fat of lambs: they shall consume; into smoke shall they consume away.'"*

Do you understand what God showed Dave here? That God will destroy the evil ones!

"Look at verses 35 and 36, *'I have seen the wicked in great power, and spreading himself like a green bay tree. Yet he passed away, and, lo, he was not: yea, I sought him, but he could not be found.'*

"I remember a number of years ago when Jimmy Hoffa was the head of the Teamsters Union. He made the Kennedys tremble. This man had such power — he paralyzed Washington D.C., and New York City with a massive truckers' strike.

"They were choking our city. I have it marked in one of my old Bibles, I put his name right by this because at that time he was spreading himself like a green bay tree. He was in great power. I said, 'Oh, God, how long do these men flaunt their power like that? The whole government is trembling.'"

SOME TIME LATER, Jimmy Hoffa went to a restaurant and disappeared. He was never seen again alive. "I remember marking the date in my Bible," said Dave.

"The Lord was giving me an illustration of the wicked in great power — and how they fall.

"By the way, where is Adolf Hitler? Where is Joseph Stalin? Where is former Soviet Premier Nikita Khruschev who declared that he would bury America and took his shoe off at the United Nations, banged it on the desk as he screamed his denunciations of us all?

"They're all gone!

"One of these days every one of these who flaunt their power will be gone, too. God says, 'I'm going to consume them.'"

What are we to do as Christians? "In this time of turmoil when everything is going crazy, our newspapers are full of the panic on all sides. But the Bible makes it very clear that you and I as Christians are to stay calm and not get hot under the collar.

"READ PSALM 37:1, *'Fret not thyself because of evildoers,'* You get your dictionary and look up the word "fret." It means don't get hot under the collar, don't grieve, don't panic as if God weren't on the throne.

"God has everything under control for the church. He always has. We are to be concerned. We are to reach out and help the lost, but we are to stay calm, we're not to react to all these devilish things as if we had no God.

"God has not been surprised by any of it. The church is never to cringe in front of anything the devil tries to flaunt at it. We are not to cringe. The church never has and never will. You know, there is nothing the devil is doing today that is going to stop God's eternal purpose.

"Nothing.

"The devil may have decided to take over the whole nations of Colombia and Burma. Did you read in the paper that there are 30,000 bodyguards in Colombia who make a full-time living protecting the judges and government officials — and some of them guard the crooks and drug lords, too?

"BUT YOU KNOW, in spite of all the turmoil in Colombia, God is in control. We have just opened a drug center there. *New Life for Girls* has just opened in Colombia, and

I got a report recently where things are starting to get on fire for God.

"Fired up Christians are going right into some of these drug hot spots and they are witnessing and preaching to the drug lords.

"And the church is growing in spite of all the drug war down there.

"The devil has tried to keep the Gospel out of Eastern Europe — but we've all seen what He has done!

"Now Teen Challenge has two centers there, one opened already in Poland, another proposed center in Hungary.

"AND I TELL YOU WHAT, there's no work of the devil that is going to hinder anything God has purposed in His mind to do. The devil decided to take over Times Square. He decided to bring every pusher in this city down here.

"He brought the pimps and the prostitutes and the pushers to flood this area. He carved out Times Square and the devil said, 'This is my seat. Nobody, nobody comes near Times Square.'

"DO YOU UNDERSTAND the significance of Times Square Church — and our people worshiping in the holiness of Jesus, right at this seat of Satan? Do you understand the spiritual significance of that? God is saying to His church that you don't have to be afraid, you don't get upset, you don't panic.

"Others can panic all around you, but don't fret because of evildoers.

"Don't fret because of pushers.

"Don't fret because of this battle around you.

"Don't get upset.

"Don't get hot under the collar.

"You say to God, 'How long will You wait to destroy these people?'"

Be patient, says Dave.

And learn a lesson from Jonah.

Jonah, if you remember, preached to Nineveh that if they didn't turn from their evil ways, that God would destroy them.

Then, he was heartbroken when these enemies of Israel listened to his warnings, repented, turned from their evil ways, fell to their knees before God — and were spared.

Jonah, if you remember, would have preferred to watch them be consumed by fire from Heaven.

So, let's not commit the same sin.

Be patient.

And pray that the fire will not fall.

Even though the evildoers all around us deserve to burn!

Chapter 22

Nineveh
on the
Hudson River

"I'VE BEEN PREACHING LATELY that I believe America has reached what I call the dread release," Dave told me. "It's past the point of no return, Nicky. Judgment is already on the land. There comes a time God says when even if these three men—Noah, Daniel and Job—were in it, 'I would not hear their prayer.'"

Why?

"Because there is a line that has been crossed. Some time ago, the Lord said 'That's it.' There is a time when God has to move on.

"There are prayer groups all over the United States. They write to me and say, 'Well, Brother Dave, why should we pray if you and others believe that the days of America are over and the judgment is at the door? Why do *you* pray?'

"We pray just like Josiah did. Josiah was told that judgment would not be stopped, but the Lord told Josiah it would be delayed during his time because Josiah's heart was right.

"We can delay judgment.

"We can't stop it.

"We can delay it for a while.

"OUR JOB NOW IS NOT to make America greater or to bring in some kind of a kingdom. Our purpose now is to raise up a remnant of people that is righteous and seeking the Lord with all its heart.

"I do have hope for the church and I'm very excited about what's happening in Times Square. I believe we're in a revival here. I encourage people to pray.

"Pray as never before. It's not going to stop judgment, but it could possibly delay things."

What about the day of Nineveh? God had judged Nineveh — and had turned His face against them and their sin.

But He sent Jonah.

And remember what happened when the people repented?

David nodded, ashen-faced.

"We don't have a chance now, Nicky. We have kicked the Lord out of everything in American society. We've become humanistic and materialistic.

"Nicky, it was not the Gospel of Jesus Christ that broke down the Berlin Wall and tore away the Iron Curtain. It was America's false gospel of materialism.

"East Germans were not fleeing so they could pray. They walked out on communism because it could not supply them with consumer goods.

"Well, it is a false message of hope.

"And the party is over, Nicky, the party is over. You can sense it here in New York.

"I stood in my pulpit right here the day before the stock market made its historic crash.

"I told my flock, 'If you want to see history made, meet me on Wall Street tomorrow.' I was there at the stock exchange when it happened. I had been warning our people for weeks to get out of the stock market.

"It was wrenching to see stockbrokers weeping and crying. Many yuppies on the sidewalk were lamenting, 'There goes my condo, there goes my yacht.'

"The Lord showed us at that time that was the wooden yoke.

"**WE ARE ON THE BRINK** of the iron yoke right now. We're at the point now where people say that it can't happen again and we've come out of all our problems — just look at how good things are!

"But God's going to get the world's attention one way or another and it's going to be pretty frightening. Pray for America. Pray for those who will remain when America is finished — England, Australia, New Zealand.

"We're in for quite a roller coaster ride yet."

Epilogue

YES, DAVID WILKERSON IS BACK, preaching, shepherding and pastoring in the heart of New York City. Come, stand with me in front of Times Square Church and talk with the folks leaving Sunday morning services.

What does Times Square Church mean to them? "My salvation," is one answer. "Four weeks ago I was in heavy drugs and living in the streets. One of the counselors brought me in and I was saved. I'm with the Lord now. If it weren't for this church I wouldn't be happy, content, saved. I have a great spiritual feeling right now and I want to devote myself for the rest of my life to our Lord. I couldn't do that in 41 years of my life. The only thing I was doing was being in the pit of hell with drugs. Times Square Church reached out."

I turn to a young adult and ask: *Would you say if it weren't for Times Square Church being here you wouldn't have gotten saved?* "I don't know that." comes the answer. "I just know I was here at the right time, walking by and one of the counselors from the church brought me in and

I felt our Lord for the first time in my life. And I was completely saved. Right now I'm in one of the shepherds' flocks — getting prepared to go to Teen Challenge. I want to devote myself to our Lord. I was a heroin addict and I attempted suicide. In four and a half years I have been drug free now."

"IF IT WEREN'T FOR THIS, I would be gone," says another former addict. "Dave, he tells the truth. He lets you know what is real. No half-stepping with him. He gives us the truth. God bless him always. I was drinking and drugging. But when I gave this all to God, I couldn't go anywhere else. Thank You God from the bottom of my heart."

One of the former addicts keeps mentioning how Dave's son, Greg, has helped him. Greg Wilkerson has an incredible shepherd's heart for the flock.

Proudly, Dave speaks of this son that he counts among his close confidants — indeed, a best friend.

"I'm excited about the relationship we have," Greg tells me. "I cherish that — but I feel proud, not for the accomplishment or the ministry but in the relationship that Dad and I have now. It's a real joy and a pleasure seeing that."

I CAN'T HELP BUT GRIN KNOWINGLY at this preacher's kid — who, as a little baby, I held in my arms and helped diaper. Was it rough being the son of such a superstar?

"I suffered through a lot of things that I brought on myself," he says earnestly. "The pressure that came was from my trying to follow in his footsteps. I think the biggest thing he taught me was how to relieve the pressure by understanding the true things of the Lord. Dad taught me not to look at the result of the ministry, but to keep my eyes and heart on Jesus — and that comes through prayer."

How does Greg see his dad?

"As an accomplisher," he says. "I see him catching the vision of the Lord. But what I treasure is the one-on-one personal time we have had together."

What about when his mother got so very ill?

"It was a very challenging time in our lives, I'll be very honest," he admits. "I can remember coming home from school at first when my mom had cancer. I would worry about that as I came in, not knowing whether she was going to be in bed or up.

"It made me grow up very fast. I would see Dad in a corner silently weeping, crying out to the Lord. I would see the hurt. It was hard."

One time in particular, Dave was absolutely crushed under the incredible burden of his wife's illness. Greg was only 10 or 11, but he remembers for the first time seeing his father absolutely broken before the Lord. He tells of comforting his dad and of the sobbing man resting his head on his little boy's shoulder. "For the first time, I began to understand my dad," Greg remembers. "I felt so responsible. It was good. I saw his heart for the first time."

What about the controversies — when so many people seemingly turned on his dad?

"I was young and not able to understand all that," he muses. "I would hear the gossip and it would cut me like a knife. It hurt. There was an anger that built within me until the Lord showed me that's not really what it's all about. And I gave up that anger. I said, 'Lord, I surely don't understand how Paul suffered.'"

IF HE HAD HIS LIFE to live over again, what would David Wilkerson do differently?

"If I had to go back and do it over again," he mused, "I would live every day, as much as I could, as if it were my last one.

"I regret the hours I spent years ago in front of the television set. I would come home from an altar call, walk in, turn on the television set and sit for two hours trying to unwind in front of the TV. I don't do that anymore. I come home after I've preached and go into my room and I enjoy His sweetness and pray for those who came to the altar. Then I get my Bible out and ask the Lord to recharge my battery.

"The most vulnerable time for a preacher is right after he's had a success or after he has ministered. Most ministers who fall sexually and morally are tempted right after a great moving of the Holy Spirit. Because they are so open, the devil sees that openness and he moves right in.

"So I make it a practice now to go home after the meetings and seek Him. I have wasted years and that hurts. I weep over that. This past week I had hours of saying, 'God, I can't believe the time I've wasted. That's one of the main reasons I preach so strongly against TV and the Christian. I don't believe a minister can keep the anointing while filling his mind with the garbage on TV.

"I don't see how it can improve anyone's mind or anything else, and I don't care who says differently. I think it's imperative for Christians who want to go all the way with the Lord to really let their TVs go.

"If they call that legalism I don't care."

HOW WOULD GREG LIKE PEOPLE to remember his dad? "As a man of God," he answers simply.

"As a man of his word," says Gwen.

"As a man of God," repeats daughter Debbie, "and that he loved his family. He was always there for all of us. I think if people really knew him as just himself, and not as

'Dave Wilkerson the evangelist,' they would see the loving, tender caring side of him. And that's what I would like people to remember."

"But I know what he would like: to know ... *that people only saw Jesus through him.*"

I thank God for Dave.

HE IS A MAN OF GOD unlike any other I have ever known. He knows God intimately. He is a student of the Word, of church history, of the writings of great men of God gone before him.

He is a man of prayer — a man who really walks with God. The diversity of the Times Square Church's ministry in New York City is amazing. Holy Spirit discernment is needed to protect the time, emotions and energies of those involved. This comes through intimacy with Christ, having His mind, seeing others through His eyes and sharing His love.

This sort of leadership and lifestyle is not learned, it is imparted by association with Jesus. Only a man who walks with God can reflect His heart. Dave reflects the heart of God — the One Hope for Mankind.

DESPITE HIS TENDENCY TO GIVE everything away, Dave is an astute businessman — by the power of the Lord. God has given him enormous favor and uncanny insights into financial matters. Just look at the beautiful auditorium he secured ... by the hand of the Lord.

Even his quiet times before the Lord are different than before. Recently as I walked with him, I saw a new peacefulness.

In the past, there was always a hyperactivity, a nervous restlessness. But now he's calmed down. And as we talked about some who have fallen away, I saw deep hurt and concern in his eyes. I saw for the first time the caring shepherd. He was listening to me as never before. He cared.

Such a shepherd! Although his church is growing, he remains available — even to the point of refusing prestigious speaking engagements. His call now is to these people. And they line up backstage to speak with their pastor after every service. Even after he has extended himself beyond his energies, he still greets and ministers to each one who needs him.

I WATCHED AS HE WAS TOUCHED by their fears and hurts. And I saw him go home and weep with Gwen for their pain, the ravages of their sin and the terrible destruction by Satan.

Is Dave the savior of New York City?

No. He has no illusions about salvaging the city, rescuing every teen-age runaway or restoring every wrecked life. But he is determined to extend his church to help as many as possible.

His mission in New York City is a life-and-death mission from the Lord. Dave respects that call and walks in holy fear to be responsible for those whom the Lord has sent him.

And his heart is newly broken.

THE WARNINGS that have characterized his life are delivered with compasion.

He is one of the most honest people I have ever known — willing to admit his mistakes and seek forgiveness.

David Wilkerson.

Pastor of Times Square Church,.

A man of God.

A husband.

A father.

A shepherd.

An evangelist.

A watchman.

Perhaps a prophet.

But the bottom line is: *David Wilkerson is a man of God.* His life has been dedicated to pointing others to Jesus Christ.

So, I would have you pause. Look at Dave's life. As you do, you may see something you've not seen before.

You may glimpse Jesus.

Shining through this mere, humble man.

"IS AMERICA TOO FAR GONE?" I asked him a few days ago. "Is it really all over? Is the situation hopeless? Can't the Lord cure our nation's wounds? He did it for Israel — 2,000 years after that nation was seemingly blotted from the face of the earth!"

"God is in control, Nicky," Dave told me, his voice low. "To America and all nations, God still says, 'Yea, I have loved thee with an everlasting love: Therefore with lovingkindness have I drawn thee' (Jer. 31:3). To wicked Israel the Lord said, 'Yet will I not make a full end of thee: but I will correct thee in measure, and will not leave thee altogether unpunished' (Jer. 30:11).

"Nicky, Israel suffered an incurable wound of sin! But there remained a people in Israel who engaged their hearts to approach the Lord. God healed Israel's incurable wound and saved a nation already under judgment! He restored it and built the city on its own heap! He multiplied and blessed them, and 'their children also shall be as aforetime' (Jer. 30:20).

"I HAVE BEEN SAYING OVER AND OVER about America what the Bible says about Israel: *The wound is incurable.*

"But God could restore America the same way He did Israel! He could heal the wasted years if He had a people engaged in seeking Him!

"He could wipe out all the years of wickedness and restore and rebuild! Scripture says God 'ransomed him from the hand of him that was stronger than he' (Jer. 31:11). He can do the same thing for America!

"Nicky, we see a picture of such restoration in the New Testament," said Dave, "when Jesus healed a man with a withered hand, 'Saith He to the man, Stretch forth thine hand. And he stretched it forth; and it was restored whole, like as the other' (Matt. 12:13)."

You see when Jesus restores you, the old wounds can't even be found!

"Yes, there is still hope.

"But time is running out."

If you would like to know more about David Wilkerson or Nicky Cruz — or would just like to make comments, feel free to write to:

Nicky Cruz Outreach
P.O. Box 25070
Colorado Springs, CO 80936